In this delightful volume, edited by Kevin Belmonte, readers get an extraordinarily intimate portrait of C.H. Spurgeon through the lens of his letters to his wife Susannah while away on his travels. The picture we get of Spurgeon from this collection is of an affectionate husband, a lover of nature, a faithful friend, a happy Christian, and a devoted worshipper of God. Along the way, we see Spurgeon's fervent piety, personal warmth, and good humor painted in vivid colors. *Letters and Travels* is a unique and welcome addition to the growing corpus of published material on the Prince of Preachers.

Alex DiPrima
Pastor, Emmanuel Church
Winston-Salem, North Carolina; Author, *Spurgeon and the Poor: How the Gospel Compels Christian Social Concern*

The Spurgeons were a most unusual couple. Not many wives would delight in reading the details of a husband's travels to beautiful and exciting places without her. But Susie keenly understood that Charles had to get away to improve his health and she was not well enough to travel with him. His careful descriptions coupled with his sweet words about missing her at every turn surely brought her joy.

The Prince of Preachers' sense of humor comes through loud and clear as does his frustration with those who practice false religions. I found myself amused to picture Charles Spurgeon as a tourist in cities I have been blessed to visit even as he meticulously noted the beauty of The Artist's created world everywhere he traveled. While we don't have access to Susie's frequent letters to Charles, it is nice to have Kevin Belmonte's well edited collection of Spurgeon's letters to her even as we marvel yet again at what a gift to the Church they both were.

Mary K. Mohler
Wife of Southern Seminary president, Albert Mohler
Author of Susannah Spurgeon, *Lessons for a Life of Joyful Eagerness in Christ*

When Susie Spurgeon compiled her husband's autobiography, she gave a gift to the church: she included her husband's daily love letters to her during his travels in England (1873) and Europe (1871). Why are these letters such a gift? Because in them we see a glimpse of Spurgeon beyond his celebrity and greatness. Here, we see Spurgeon in his humanity, resting and recovering from the rigors of ministry. In a day when pastors are burned out and Christians are weary, these letters are a reminder that rest is God's good gift. In his travels, Spurgeon models for us how we can enjoy God's world in our rest with childlike faith and wonder, and so, be energized and equipped for faithful service.

Geoff Chang
Assistant Professor of Historical Theology
Curator of the Spurgeon Library, Midwestern Baptist
Theological Seminary

What a wonderful addition to Kevin Belmonte's fine books! I can't recommend his work highly enough.

Michael D. McMullen
Professor of Church History,
Midwestern Baptist Theological Seminary

Letters and Travels

by C.H. Spurgeon

Edited by Kevin Belmonte

CHRISTIAN
FOCUS

Copyright © Edited by Kevin Belmonte 2023

hardback ISBN 978-1-5271-1050-2
ebook ISBN 978-1-5271-1108-0

10 9 8 7 6 5 4 3 2 1

Published in 2023
by
Christian Focus Publications Ltd,
Geanies House, Fearn, Ross-shire,
IV20 1TW, Great Britain.

www.christianfocus.com

Cover design by Pete Barnsley

Printed by Gutenberg, Malta

Spurgeon image source: the frontispiece photograph from
C.H. Spurgeon's Autobiography, volume 3,
(London: Passmore & Alabaster, 1899)

Contents

~ Dedication ~

... to the memory of Susannah Spurgeon,
whose literary labour gave the reflections set down in
these pages ...

৯৵৵৵৵৶

He who forgets ... the song of birds in the wood, the rippling of rills among the rushes, and the sighing of the wind among the pines, needs not wonder if his heart forgets to sing and his soul grows heavy. A day's breathing of fresh air upon the hills, or a few hours' ramble ... the new-mown hay, and the fragrant hops — these are the best medicines ... the best refreshments for the weary.[1]

Flashes of Thought (1874)

I have also been up St. Giles' Hill, above Winchester, and watched the setting sun, and have seen the lamps lit one after another, all along the hill. It was very beautiful indeed, and the evening was so cool and calm. It did me a world of good ...[2]

A Letter Home to Clapham (1873)

---

1. C.H. Spurgeon, *Flashes of Thought* (London: Passmore & Alabaster, 1874), 450.
2. *C.H. Spurgeon's Autobiography, v. 3* (London: Passmore & Alabaster, 1899), 262-263.

In the forest.
A scene from Spurgeon's holiday, as shown in his *Autobiography*.

☙ FOREWORD ❧

Spurgeon commanded the pulpit like none other in his day. His oratory magic found its way into the hands of an even wider audience through his pen. Spurgeon's command of language and turns of phrase captured the hearts and minds of audiences globally in his day and reaches well into our own with the printed page.

But this is where we often leave Spurgeon—aloft in his pulpit, Bible in hand, teaching the Scriptures.

This volume is a rare treat in that it captures a different side of the famed preacher. In these pages, we find a Spurgeon on repose—a Spurgeon refreshing himself in the glories of nature and connecting with the wonders of the Creator he so lovingly preached. Forests, fields, flowers, and countryside work together to create a tapestry of beauty in Spurgeon's own reflections. His delight in the beauty of horses and even the variegated uniqueness of different trees is captured here in a glorious fashion.

But it's not just nature. As Spurgeon travels to Rome and Italy, he chronicles his awe and wonder at the classical buildings and sites in the same ways pilgrims to these places respond in our own day.

This book pulls together classic images and a wide variety of sources to help the modern reader connect with Spurgeon's wonderment on a personal level. The inclusion of his wife Susannah's own reflections drives this home so well. Even in his final days, Spurgeon's thoughts and reflections from the south of France demonstrate his love for his Creator.

In reading this volume by Spurgeon scholar, Kevin Belmonte, one cannot help but be reminded of William Cowper's famed verse, *The Task*. In this poem, Cowper masterfully carries the balance of delight in the traveller's task:

> None more admires, the painter's magic skill,
> Who shows me that which I shall never see,
> Conveys a distant country into mine,
> And throws Italian light on English walls.
> But imitative strokes can do no more
> Than please the eye, sweet Nature every sense.
> The air salubrious of her lofty hills,
> The cheering fragrance of her dewy vales,
> And music of her woods — no works of man
> May rival these; these all bespeak a power
> Peculiar, and exclusively her own.
> Beneath the open sky she spreads the feast;
> 'Tis free to all — 'tis ev'ry day renewed,
> Who scorns it, starves deservedly at home.[1]

---

1. William Cowper, *The Task and Other Poems*, ed. Henry Morley (London: Cassell and Company, 1899).

Spurgeon was not one to starve at home. Hopefully, neither are we.

May readers of this volume be encouraged to mimic Spurgeon's insatiable delight and wonderment at the works of the Creator and the world the Saviour redeemed.

John Mark Yeats
Vice President of Student Services
Dean of Students and Professor of Church History
Midwestern Baptist Theological Seminary
and Spurgeon College

❧ A WORD OF INTRODUCTION ☙

For all the works of art that Spurgeon saw in the great museums of Europe, and they many times captured his imagination, none surpassed the beauty, majesty, or awesome power he saw written in creation.

The Lord was, to use his phrase, 'the Great Artist.' Spurgeon revelled in that, and his profound gratitude for this side of God's character has much to teach us.

At the same time, for all his life, and very genuinely, Spurgeon loved history, art, architecture, and literary scenes. He thanked God for days of sojourn he had among places of culture, when rest and renewal were needed to husband and restore his health, as well as his spirit. This is telling. He was a student of the many lessons history, art, architecture, and literary scenes have to teach us—we do well to be such students also. For otherwise, we miss much that inspires.

My hope, as editor of the writings that follow, is to commend the good things in all that Spurgeon has written here.

Whether readers here are pastors, or those who listen to sermons from Sunday to Sunday, there is a need to know the importance and meaning Spurgeon attached to seasons of rest, renewal, and holidays away with friends or family.

At such times, we're reminded that a loving God gives them to us, for our blessing—as a season when we learn things of Him that renew, and enrich, the days of service that He calls us to.

Kevin Belmonte
Woodholme
Summer 2022

≈ PREFACE FOR THE SUMMER HOLIDAY WRITINGS, 1873 ≈

One of Spurgeon's 'most congenial recreations' was spending 'a long day in the country, driving over hill and dale,' in the 'charming county' of Surrey. As his wife Susannah recalled, 'many sweet days of rest' were thus 'snatched from weeks of heavy toil, and a furlough of a few hours … helped to restore and refresh.'

For these occasions, Spurgeon went 'in good time, taking with him some choice companion, or, perchance, another weary worker; and, driving slowly, they would jog along till noon, when, at a pleasant wayside inn, they would rest the horse, and have their luncheon, returning in the cool of the evening for high tea … at 6 or 7 o'clock.' Such rest was a gift; but it was 'surpassed, and completed, when a fortnight of similar days could be linked together to form a perfect holiday.'

For then, instead of driving back in the sunset, Spurgeon's trip 'would extend itself to many towns.' On these excursions, Susannah said, 'his ideas of comfort, and his disregard of external appearances, were equally conspicuous. He liked a cosy seat, and easy travelling;

but he cared nothing for the style of his equipage:—an old horse—most inappropriately named 'Peacock,'—and a shabby carriage, were matters of perfect indifference to him; so long as they were safe and trustworthy, and carried him out of the noise of the crowded world into the stillness and beauty of nature's quiet resting-places.' Indeed Spurgeon had purchased, for these rambles, 'a vehicle of so antiquated a pattern, and of such unfashionable proportions,' that it was immediately dubbed 'Punch's coach,' and ever after bore that name.

A travelling carriage, of the kind used in Spurgeon's time.

When 'packed and prepared for a journey,' its overstuffed set of luggage 'added exceedingly to its grotesque and inelegant appearance.' Yet far from a nuisance, this 'convenient provision' was, in Spurgeon's estimation, 'one of its chief advantages.'

More than a few times, Susannah Spurgeon 'laughed afresh' at the sight of this carriage, but she loved the sight of her husband's 'beaming ... satisfied face, as he started off on one of these country tours.' That recollection was 'far more deeply impressed' on her than the remembrance of his 'unsightly holiday caravan.'

And truly, Spurgeon was 'never more happy and exultant than when making excursions of this kind.' Those privileged to accompany him 'saw him at his social best;' and with one accord, they testified to 'the charm of his companionship.'

So to the reason for this book. From Spurgeon's daily letters to his wife, 'on one of these notable occasions,' it's possible to weave the story of his holiday drive into a personal narrative, setting forth traits in his character 'which could in no other way have been so naturally revealed.' These were his 'intense delight in the works of God, his fine appreciation of the minute, or half-concealed lovelinesses of nature, his care for all living creatures, [and] his calm and contented spirit.' All these, as Susannah said, are cast in distinct relief 'by the lively touches of his own vigorous pen.'

One further word remains …

During the holiday described in the pages to follow, the 'old horse' mentioned above, 'Peacock,' who 'made so many delightful journeys,' was not pressed into service. Rather, the 'noble greys' referred to in the opening sentences of Spurgeon's letters were a team 'owned and driven by a member of the party.' All the same, these noble greys were harnessed, just as Peacock had been, to draw 'Punch's coach.'

That made for a colourful and memorable occasion all its own.[1]

---

1. All quotes in this Preface are taken from *C.H. Spurgeon's Autobiography. vol. 3* (London: Passmore & Alabaster, 1899), 258-259.

PART ONE

AN ENGLISH SUMMER
HOLIDAY, 1873

❧ THE HOLIDAY BEGINS ❧

I was sitting, one day, in the New Forest, under a beech tree. I like to look at the beech, and study it, as I do many other trees, for every one has its own peculiarities and habits, its special ways of twisting its boughs, and growing its bark, and opening its leaves, and so forth. As I looked up at that beech, and admired the wisdom of God in making it, I saw a squirrel running round and round the trunk, and up the branches, and I thought to myself:

'Ah! this beech tree is a great deal more to you than it is to me, for it is your home, your living, your all.'

Its big branches were the main streets of his city, and its little boughs were the lanes; somewhere in that tree he had his house, and the beech-mast was his daily food, he lived on it. Well, now, the way to deal with God's Word is not merely to contemplate it, or to study it, as a student does— but to live on it, as that squirrel lives on his beech tree. Let it be to you, spiritually, your house, your home, your food, your medicine, your clothing: the one essential element of your soul's life and growth.

— 'Living on the Word,' (15 March 1883)

Spurgeon was, to cite the old phrase, 'a man of many parts.' One lifelong, but lesser-known side of his character was a love of nature, and time in the country. He owned many books about the natural world, flora and fauna, and he knew Gilbert White's classic text, *The Natural History and Antiquities of Selbourne*, well. Indeed, he was so fond of this book that he made retracing places White described a highlight of his summer holiday in 1873. So it is in this context that the letters about his summer journey commence …

৯৯৯৯

Alton.—June, 1873. I am having a grand time. The horses are noble greys; the carriage, with my luggage-basket behind, most comfortable. We go along with an ease and dignity seldom equalled, and never surpassed.

From Guildford, we drove to the foot of Martha's Chapel, and climbed to the very summit. What a view! Then down, and back to Guildford, and up the Hog's Back. Mistaking the route, we went up an old deserted Roman road, immensely broad, and all green.

What a piece of country! The road itself was a sight, and the views on either side were sublime. So on to Farnham, where we dined, and went into the Bishop's park, which you will remember, with its deer, and avenue of elms.

From Farnham to Alton is pretty and fruitful, but there were no incidents [to tell about]. I revised part of a sermon last night, and went to bed at 11:30; fell asleep at once, and neither stirred nor dreamed. I awoke at 6:00, then got up, and finished the sermon. Already, I am so much better that I feel able to go to work again,—quite.

The market town of Farnham, near the close of the 1800s.

We go to Selbourne this afternoon. How I wish you were with me! But you shall know anything I see, which can help you to realize where I am, and what I am doing.

By the way, this morning we went into the church here, and saw an old door which was riddled by the Parliamentarians [during the Civil War in Cromwell's time]; we were also regaled with a superabundance of organ music which a young gentleman volunteered. The church is restored very beautifully, and in good taste.

ฺ๛๛๛

Same day, later. The drive was delicious, and I feel so well. Selbourne is a little heaven of delights. It is Switzerland in miniature, where every turn changes the scene.

If it were in a foreign land, all the world would crowd to it. We were all charmed; who could be otherwise? Well might [Gilbert] White write so prettily upon so choice a subject. Hill, dell, bourne, hanger, down, lane, and wood,—one has them all within a very small compass, and with endless variety.

We have returned to Alton to send off some of our party; and now, at a council of war, we have decided to visit Selbourne again to-morrow, and see more of that gem of a village.

The Hanger, Selbourne, from *Hampshire, with the Isle of Wight* (1901).

Selbourne.—what a grand morning we have had! Up the Hanger, above the village, we climbed by a zigzag path, and had a very extensive view.

It was delicious to ramble among the tall beeches, and peep down upon the village, and then to descend into

The Wakes, naturalist Gilbert White's home.

the place itself by winding paths. We went to [Gilbert] White's house, and were received very kindly by Professor Bell and his wife, both very agèd persons. We were soon known, and had in honour …

We rambled about as in a paradise, and then were off to Alresford.

What enjoyment I have had, and what health is upon me! I never felt better in my life. We are all so happy with the scenery, that we do not know how to be grateful enough. Oh, that you were here!

Alresford, as shown in John Duthy's *Sketches of Hampshire* (1839).

One of these days, I hope and pray you may be able to come.

From Alresford, we have driven here (Winchester), along the beautiful valley of the Itchen, and your dear note was all I wanted to make me full of joy. Letters had accumulated here up to Wednesday. I have already answered twenty-five ...

✽ OF ANCIENT TIME, AND SCENES ✾

Winchester is a rare old place. We went first to the Hospital of St. Cross, and had a piece of bread, and a cup of beer. The cups are of horn, with five silver crosses on them; and my trio of friends bought one for me as a souvenir, and present for my coming birthday ...

Brethren of St. Cross.

Having tasted of the hospitality of St. Cross, we passed into its rectangle, under the arch of the Beaufort Tower.

Beaufort Tower and Hall of St. Cross.

It is here that the 'dole' is given, and here we saw some of the old brethren in their gowns with crosses; there are thirteen of these old pensioners, and they get two quarts of beer to drink every day, and on 'gaudy days' gin and beer hot! Indeed, these old Saxon institutions appear to have regarded beer as the grand necessary of life!

We walked and talked, and then sat down on the steps leading up into the dining-hall, and quietly looked on the curious scene. In the days when the place was built, chimneys were a new invention, and therefore they are all external, and have a grotesque appearance. On one side are the cloisters, and at the further end is a noble church, in which service is performed twice a day.

Our next visit was to St. Catherine's Hill, but as I could not pretend to climb it, we kept along the river-bank till

The Dole at St. Cross Hospital, Winchester.

we reached the cathedral. Here, a most intelligent guide made a couple of hours pass away as if they had only been so many minutes. I know more about architecture now than I had ever imagined I could learn, and am able to talk quite fluently about Early English, Decorated, Norman, etc., etc. It was strange to see the chests in which were the bones of Edgar, Ethelwulf, and all those old Saxon kings, and the sarcophagus of William Rufus. There is a kaleidoscopic window, all of the true old material, but no design, order, or arrangement; it reminded me of some men's theological knowledge,—their system is of the 'anyhow' character.

The thing which pleased us most was a pulpit, into which I ascended. The whole place was full of interest, even down to the crypt, into which we ventured.

Winchester College, Hampshire, founded by William Wykeham in 1382.

After the cathedral, we visited the famous school of William Wykeham, where the 'tunding' took place. It is like one of the Cambridge Colleges, and very quaint are its ways. The photograph I send you shows the tower of the school-chapel, and the Quakers'-meeting-looking place in front is the French school.

We saw the dining-hall, and the great buttery hatches through which the meat and beer are passed, of which the boys have as much as they choose;—Saxon again! Near the kitchen, is the ancient painting of 'the faithful servant,' which seems to be held in high repute at Winchester, but I think it a very poor thing.

I have also been up St. Giles' Hill, above Winchester, and watched the setting sun, and have seen the lamps lit one after another all along the hill. It was very beautiful

Wotton Hatch, a favourite resting-place of Mr. Spurgeon.

indeed, and the evening was so cool and calm it did me a world of good.

Salisbury.—To-day has been very dull and wet. Our drive through Hursley to Romsey was all very well; but from Romsey here, there was a constant downpour, and it got to be rather wearisome. It rains still, and I feel very tired; but a sunny day to-morrow will set me up again. I don't like big hotels in towns, like dear old 'Hatches,' and the blessèd trees.

Amesbury.—Sabbath. Last evening, we went into the grounds of the Abbey Park, the property of Sir Edward Antrobus. The River Avon runs through the domain; in many windings, branchings, and twistings. The grounds are thickly wooded, but so little frequented that we heard

Amesbury and the River Avon.

the hoarse crow of the pheasant, the coo of pigeons, the cry of waterfowl, the song of countless birds, and the plash of leaping fish, but no sound of man's profaning footsteps. We sat on an ornamental bridge, and listened to the eloquence of nature, while the river hastened along beneath us.

> In this parish are two chalk hills very conspicuous from the railway, S., one of which, *Sidon Hill* (940 ft.), is the highest ground in Hampshire. The other, *Beacon Hill*, rises to 900 ft. Noble views are commanded from both. "From these hills you look at one view over the whole of Berkshire, into Oxfordshire, Gloucestershire, and Wiltshire, and you can see the Isle of Wight and the sea. On the N. side the chalk soon ceases, the sand and clay begin, and the oak woods cover a great part of the surface."—*Cobbett*, 'Rural Rides.'

Beacon Hill, as described in *A Handbook for Travellers in Surrey, Hampshire, and the Isle of Wight* (1858).

The family being away, we had leave to wander anywhere, and we enjoyed the liberty very much. I was up this morning at six o'clock, dressing slowly, and meditating; then I came down, and had an hour's work at The Interpreter. I do not mean to preach to-day, except with my pen; and it is a great pleasure to me to use that instrument when thought flows freely.

May you also have a quiet day, and gather strength! May the Lord God of Israel bless my own best-beloved, and cause His face to shine upon her!

৩৵৵৵

We had a nice little service yesterday morning, and after dinner, we went into the woods again. How I wished you could have been with me!

Imagine a series of cathedrals of beech trees; the pillars all of silver, and the roof of emerald lacework and twinkling stars of sunlight; the walls of dense yew trees, and the floor ankle-deep of red and brown leaves, softer than a velvet carpet. Rain fell; but, under the yews, we only heard it patter; and as we lay still, we could hear the wild ducks on the stream, far down below, making love, and war.

Presently, the sun came out, and we walked through the grand avenues up to a hill, which stood as a cliff above the Avon, with the Abbey House full in view, and Beacon Hill and the Wiltshire range of Downs with plentiful tumuli.

Here again we saw pheasants in the mead on the other side, one white one among them, and wild ducks and coots on the river, diving, swimming, and flying after one another. Swallows were all around us. Wood-pigeons came every now and then, and some were in the trees cooing constantly.

Hawks poised themselves in the air, flocks of starlings flew overhead, like November meteors, thrushes and blackbirds sang; and, last of all, there came, on downy yellow pinions, white-breasted and round-faced, your friend the owl, who sped into the wood, and was soon followed by another, whose soft course, on noiseless broad-sailing wings, would have made you nestle up to me for joy, and whisper:

'Oh, husband, how lovely!'

All the while, the fish leaped as if they were quite at home, for we were as high above them and all the other things as if we were on a church spire. We then walked down green alleys, and started the rabbits in families; and, as we stood still, we saw their gambols, and marked the hares sitting upright, so that, seeing only their backs, they might have been mistaken for stumps of trees, if it had not been for their ears.

I send you a sketch of them. A sneeze made them run, or rather, leap away. Then we came on young partridges and hen-coops, which we left at once, for fear of offending; and so came in to tea, walking along the river-bank, and smelling the new mown hay. It was a sweet Sabbath. To-day and yesterday, I have done twenty-four pages of The Interpreter, and have sixteen more to do when I can. Love as deep as the sea and as broad, I send thee, my dear one.

⚘ PICTURES, PARKS, AND VILLAGES ☞

Lyndhurst. Three dainty notes [from you] have I devoured; real delicacies, flavoured with the love I prize above all earthly things.

This place is so beautiful that, to linger here for a week or two, will be delightful, and better than going elsewhere. On the way here, we drove to Broadlands,[1] and had a good view of the interior. There is as fine a collection of pictures as I ever saw, distributed over a house replete with comforts and conveniences. The Temples and Palmerstons were set forth in noble portraits, but there were many works of Sir Joshua Reynolds, Sir Peter Lely, Wouvverman, and other great masters; many Dutch pictures, and a large number full of interest, and truly instructive works of art.

A mile further, we saw Embley Park, where Miss Nightingale was born, and another four or five miles brought us into the forest amid the wildest scenery, and boundless wildernesses of shade.

---

1. Broadlands, the English country home of Baron Mount-Temple in Spurgeon's time. A devout Christian, the Baron often held public prayer meetings there.

The grounds of Embley Park, the birthplace and home of
Florence Nightingale.

Here we came upon Rufus Stone, of which I send you
all three sides. I bought them of a poor boy in a smock-
frock, on the spot. *'Mother paints 'em, Sor,'* was the answer
of this youth to my question, *'Where do you buy them?'*
What are the Selbornians after, to have no photographs
of their sweet village?

… how vivid history becomes when such memorials
are before one's eyes! The top of the iron pillar is grated,
so that we could look in, and see the stone which it
encases. Here it began to rain, but we had only about
four miles to drive to Lyndhurst; so we went along very
gently, in alternate shower and shine.

So ends this week's chronicle.

I do not think more could well have been seen;
certainly, more could not be enjoyed by any living man
in the absence of a dear wife to share his pleasure. How
I should have loved you to have seen the partridges, and
rabbits, and birds of all kinds, and forest trees and cedars,

36

and roses and honeysuckles! It may yet be. The Lord cheer thy heart ... dearest among women! Accept my most fervent love ...

Yesterday morning, we went for a ride through 'The Manor,' and there we came upon a very Atlantic of rhododendrons! Huge billows of these flowers dashed up into the trees, or sank into deep hollows, and that for a mile or so in length, and a quarter of a mile in depth. The azaleas and rarer rhododendrons are past, but enough remained to make a matchless sea of colour and beauty. How I wished you were there!

Thence we drove to Castle Malwood, where Rufus slept the night before he was shot. It stands on a round hill, and the owner has cut out openings in the wood, so as to give a series of glorious views. It is like a circular picture-gallery; for, looking through a frame of green, you see the towns and villages far away. None but a man of taste would have thought of such a thing, and carried it out so well.

New Forest, near Castle Malwood, in the late 1800s.

Some of the views are wonderful; no artist could copy them, they are so far away, yet so large and so full of detail. In the afternoon, clouds hung low, there was no air, all was close and thundery; our heads ached, and though we went out for a walk, we could scarcely breathe.

Sabbath.—I have been to the little Baptist Chapel, and have been much refreshed with a plain sermon from [the text,] *'Master, carest Thou not that we perish?'*

We then walked in the wood, and talked and meditated. It is a grand thing to be lost in the forest, within five minutes of coming out of a meeting-house!

৵৵৵৵

Monday. This morning, we have been in the forest again from ten till twelve. There are great masses of beech in one place, then oak, then underwood and small trees. Amid these are green lawns, and verdant valleys, glades, dells, hills, and vales. Sometimes, trees disappear, and all is common, with gorse, heather, and low bushes. Cottages surprise you everywhere, in nooks as secret as the haunts of fairies. Cattle with bells create an Alpine tinkling, horses and hogs go in troops.

Everything is picturesque, and the space seems boundless. One might soon be lost, for the roads, and tracks, and mere trails, are countless. Birds and insects abound, and wild flowers and mosses. It is a world of beauty, I can say no less.

The trunks of the stately trees, all aglow with lichen and moss, are loveliness itself; and the weird oaks are sometimes grotesque, and at other times solemn.

The Hill Woods, Lyndhurst.

Lyndhurst is only a village, but it is in the forest, and that is its charm. You can ramble where you will, and no man can threaten you for trespassing.

We hoped to see some of the fallow deer, and the squirrels; but have not succeeded as yet. We tracked a little brawling brook this morning; and if ever perfect beauty has existed on earth since the Fall, we saw it.

What with foxgloves on the banks, and rare ferns at the river's brim and the rippling waters among mossy mole-mounds, and thyme-bearing knolls, and the red floor beneath the temple of beech shade,—it was matchless!

I am as happy as half a being can be without the other half! It would be bliss, indeed, if you were here to share my joys.

❧ TO BE NOURISHED BY COUNTRY FACT ❧

Tuesday. An evening drive has been supremely delightful from its coolness, and from the shadows and the gleams of glory from the setting sun, which here and there lit up the tree-tops, blazed among the old roots, and gilded the lofty forest columns. I feel as peaceful as serenity itself.

No place upon earth could so fitly minister to a wearied brain by giving such perfect rest. It is better than cities, pictures, or even mountains, for all is peace, and there is not even sublimity to excite the emotions of the mind.

One rests, and gazes on a spider's web all silvered o'er, and set with diamonds of dew; a beetle flying heavily; a dragon-fly dashing forward like a cavalier charging the foe, then hesitating and irresolute until another fit of energy seizes him; a foal frisking with delight at its mother's side; a snake rustling hurriedly away among the red leaves, or a partridge scurrying across the heather! Thank God for such peaceful scenes!

We have been through Bolder Wood and Mark Ash, and seen the most wonderful forest scenery I have ever beheld or even dreamed of.

The huge beeches and oaks are so fantastic as to seem grotesque and wizard-like. They are beyond measure marvellous, and one could visit them twelve times a day, and yet not see half their beauties.

Mark Ash, New Forest.

The most singular thing of all is the flying buttress of the beech trees, which I never observed before. A long bough will be supported by another which joins it from lower down, and grows into it, so as to hold it up.

This habit in the beech leads to great curiosities of growth, for there are sometimes threefold bracings, and great branches will be thus locked together, while, in other instances, one bough will curl under another in order, apparently, to hold it up. There are shapes most unshapely, and twistings most queer and unexpected, but the one object appears to be to buttress one another, and contribute to each other's strength by this strange interlacing. Just so should believers aid one another; are they not all branches of one tree?

Another place we have visited during the week is Beaulieu Abbey, which is all in ruins, but some remarkable parts remain, and the foundations of the buildings are marked out on the turf by a sort of stone edging, so that one can, in imagination, restore the whole structure.

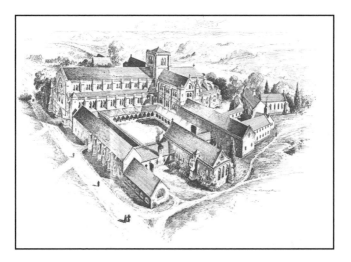

An artist's reconstruction of Beaulieu Abbey, from 1911.

We amused ourselves by trying to decipher the inscription on a broken memorial stone, but could not succeed. What a blessing to have a complete Revelation, or we should be spelling out the meaning of what we could see, and losing ourselves in endless speculation as to what might have been written on the lost fragment! I am better and better, and all the ocean of my love is yours.

A MILESTONE AND KEEPSAKE

June 19, 1873. This is my thirty-ninth birthday, and I desire to bless God for sparing and blessing me, and for giving me, as one of His choicest gifts, my own dear, precious wife. May we be spared to one another for many a day, and dwell together for ever hereafter! Thank you for your dear fond letter. Truly, it is sweet to be so dearly loved, and to love in return with an eagerness which could understand limping expressions, much more the tender words which you employ. God bless thee!

It has rained all day, so we have all been to be photographed, gratifying our vanity, since we could not indulge our observation. I am promised a copy of the group to-night before this is posted, though it will not have been long enough in water to prevent its fading; but if it pleases you for a moment, it will answer my purpose.

What do you think of your old 'hub' in the forest? Does he not look calm and happy? I think the old log just suits him, and the shabby old coat, too! I like the photograph better than any portrait ever taken of me; I wonder if you will?

જાજીઝી

Spurgeon on his thirty-ninth Birthday.

After I wrote to you yesterday, I worked a little while at The Interpreter, but soon felt one of my old attacks [of malaise] coming on, so we set off for a long walk, and at some time past ten o'clock at night we lost our way in the thick of the forest, only we knew the direction of Lyndhurst by the chimes. After breaking through the long grass, brambles, bracken, and underwood, we came to the edge of the dense enclosed wood in which we had been wandering, but a ditch and a pond barred our way.

However, there were some rails of fencing across, and over this we climbed, and went along it above the water.

We landed in a field of high grass, and made tracks for a cottage, got into the garden, down the path, and out at the front gate, nobody challenging us. This adventure did me good, and procured me a fair night's sleep.

To-day, we have been to look at the scene of our night wandering, and to find out where we missed our way. We have roamed in the wood for two hours, and have never seen a soul. Birds, rabbits, flies, ants, and spiders have been our only company—save the One with whom we have held sweet converse, and of whose Word we have spoken to each other.

✎ OVER TO A FAMOUS ISLE ✎

We have been for a drive to Lymington. It was charming to pass through the forest. Each road has its own character, and there is no sameness ...

Lymington is quite a considerable place, but I could not get a good photograph of it for you. We went down to the quay, and took the steamboat to Yarmouth in the Isle of Wight. It was about thirty minutes' steaming, and we saw Hurst Castle and the Needles to the right of us.

The Needles in 1869.

Yarmouth is a poor little place, but we walked along the beach, and sat down for a while, and enjoyed the lovely view. Fine yachts went sailing by, and porpoises were in great plenty. After being kept in by the wet, the lovely weather of to-day is doubly pleasing. Returning to Lymington at seven o'clock, we then drove back to Lyndhurst, where I found a very specially sweet note from my beloved awaiting me.

Yarmouth Square, on the Isle of Wight, circa 1900.

I am so glad you like the photo [I had taken]. It gives me real delight to afford you pleasure. I feel wonderfully well. My precious one, may the Lord give thee restoration also,[1] and make thee happy with me in journeys yet to be planned! How I should rejoice to show you about this grand forest, the noblest in all England!

---

1. An indication Susannah Spurgeon had been unwell, and was not to travel with her husband, as he wished. Sadly, due to sickness, she was sometimes an invalid.

Yesterday afternoon was spent most deliciously. We drove along the Christ-Church Road, and took the photographer and his apparatus with us, hoping to secure some charming pictures. Our purpose was, however, thwarted by the absence of the sun, for he kept behind a cloud. We then sent back the carriage, and followed on foot the little brook called the Millifont, in all its winding ways.

Ah! my darling, what choice bits we came across! Here, the water had worn out the earth from under the trees, and left bare a wattling of roots; there, in another place, clustered the water-lilies, and the green leaves with which they paved the brook. At one moment, we were on a sand island in the middle of the rivulet; at another, the bank was high above the water, like the Rhine hills, in miniature, above that mighty flood.

Strange moths and dragon-flies frequented the pools and lakelets, and here and there a fish leaped out, while shoals of minnows flashed away when our shadows fell upon them. We crossed the current upon a single fir tree, rough and unsquared; if we had tumbled into the water, it would not have mattered much, except that we could not quickly have changed our clothes.

All this walk was in solitude, among great trees. It was so singular to sit down in the silence, broken only by the warble of the brook's liquid notes, or by the noise of a moving bird, or the scream of a water-fowl, or the surprise of hearing a great crack, such as furniture will give in certain weathers.

A dog saluted us with pertinacious barking, and we found his mistress, an artist, sitting down on a sandbank in the stream, sketching. The dog evidently felt that he was her protector, but I do not think we should have seen the lady if he had not called our attention to her presence. Oh! it was delicious to lie on a bed of moss, beneath a shady beech, with ferns and foxgloves all around, and the water rippling at one's feet!

It was balm and cordial to me.

≈ FINAL STAGES OF THE JOURNEY ≈

Bishop's Waltham.[1] We left delightful Lyndhurst at about nine o'clock this morning, and drove along a charming road till we reached Southampton, and crossed by the horse-ferry to go to Netley, and explore the ruins of its Abbey.

Netley Abbey — The Cloister Court.

---

1. A medieval market town, some twelve miles south-east of Winchester.

Certainly, no place could be more congenial for an hour or so of rest. One can clamber up to the top in some places, especially in the South transept, where there is a walk on a sort of narrow ledge under the arches below the window. I was greatly interested, but could only keep on saying to myself, 'How I wish my dear wifey were here!'

From there we went to see the Victoria Hospital, driving along by the edge of Southampton Water,— such a fine drive! The Hospital is the longest building in England; I should think it is nearly half a mile long. Then we went over the hills to Botley, where the views are boundless, and so on to this queer old town. We have been wandering among the ruins of a castle-palace, where Henry II and Coeur-de-Lion have feasted in the days gone by. It has been a cool, lovely day, and the way splendid.

જ૰જ૰જ

Liphook.—We left Waltham this morning, and drove along a ridge which gave us glorious views. We turned off the good roads, and made for Winchester Hill, a great Roman or British earthwork upon an eminence. The tradition is that Winchester once stood here, but I cannot believe it. On the vast Down there are several tumuli; indeed, in the region we traversed to-day, tumuli are as plentiful as blackberries.

What air we breathed! How fresh it blew up from the sea! It was a fair requital for the puffing which it cost me to climb the hill! Then we came down to East Meon, where is an ancient church, and then we traversed a long valley between two great ranges of Downs. Such exquisite views! Nobody need go to Switzerland for the

The Anchor, Liphook.

sublime! At Petersfield, I found a sweet note from my darling. May all God's blessings be heaped upon her! As the way had been too short for a day's journey, we came on to Liphook this evening, and saw gems of views, which filled us with admiration.

Here is a great inn, of ancient date, stately and roomy. It is mentioned by old Pepys [in his diary]; but since the coaching days, its glories have departed, though it still remains comfortable and vast. I am now looking forward to my work, and hope to keep on for a long time.

Ockley.—We strolled into the park, and sat on a fallen tree.

Presently, a squirrel came and peeped at us, and not knowing our faces, he scudded away, and went up a beech. Anon he came down again, waving his tail on high, and passed us to another tree.

Then came a doe and fawn, and stood and stared; and others followed, and in Indian file went slowly off. It became cold, so we trotted in to tea; and this done, I pen a line to my darling, almost the last she will get before my return.

'The Red Lion' Inn, at Ockley, where Mr Spurgeon was a frequent visitor and where much of 'John Ploughman's Talk' was written.

A dear little note has just come from you, and rejoiced my heart. What joy to meet my beloved again, and find her better!

On Sunday, we went and sat with the Quakers, and created an event. A portly female was moved to speak, and also to admonish us against water-baptism: She was one of the old school, and evidently, relieved her soul by her exhortation.

In the afternoon, we had a fine storm and refreshing rain, and I revised a sermon, and wrote on a Psalm. Receive a great flood-tide of love from my heart to yours. May God bless us in returning to each other's beloved society, and spare us for many years to one another![2]

---

2. The entire text of this summer 1873 'travelogue' is taken from C.H. Spurgeon's *Autobiography, vol. 3* (London: Passmore & Alabaster, 1899), 259-272.

PART TWO

A CONTINENTAL HOLIDAY,
1871

✒ A TRAVELLER'S LETTER'S HOME ✒
from Susannah Spurgeon's Introduction[1]

The port city of Naples and Mount Vesuvius, seen in Spurgeon's tour of Europe, 1871, a detail from the watercolour painting presented to him by Dr. F.J. Jobson, 'in remembrance of travels in Italy.'

EDITOR'S NOTE: Though Spurgeon kept on with pastoral work in summer 1871, 'preaching once on each Sunday through August, a real holiday was essential if his health was to be re-established before the chill and damp of winter aggravated his complaint' [of gout]. So in November he left for Italy. And, as it was remembered:

---

1. Edited for ease of reading and narrative flow.

'Great was his pleasure in exploring Rome, Naples and Pompeii. More important for the future course of his life, he learned the practical lesson that if his work in London was to continue, then winter visits to the warmth and sunshine of the Mediterranean would need to become a regular event.'

However his wife Susannah, who'd been his 'delighted companion on earlier visits to the Continent, could no longer be with him,' as she explained in the lines that follow.

In 1868, my travelling days were done. Henceforth, for many years, I was a prisoner in a sick-chamber, and my beloved had to leave me when the strain of his many labours and responsibilities compelled him to seek rest far away from home.

These separations were very painful to hearts so tenderly united as were ours; but we each bore our share of the sorrow, softened as far as possible by constant correspondence.

'God bless you,' he wrote once, 'and help you to bear my absence. Better that I should be away well, than at home suffering,—better to your loving heart, I know. Do not fancy, even for a moment, that absence could make our hearts colder …

My sense of your value, and experience of your goodness, are now united to the deep passion of love which was there at the first alone. Every year casts out another anchor to hold me … though none was needed, even from the first.

May my own Lord, whose chastening hand has necessitated this absence, give you a secret inward recompense in soul, and also another recompense in the healing of the body! All my heart remains in your keeping.'

Susannah then continued:

It is marvellous to me, as I survey the yearly packets of letters which are now such precious treasures, how my husband could have managed, amidst the bustle and excitement of foreign travel, to have written so much, and so often. I many times begged him to spare himself in this matter, but he constantly assured me that it delighted him to do it:

'Every word I write is a pleasure to me, as much as ever it can be to you; it is only a lot of odds and ends I send you, but I put them down as they come, so that you may see it costs me no labour, but is just a happy scribble. Don't fret because I write you so many letters, it is such a pleasure to tell out my joy.'

'Every day,' Susannah said, 'dear messages came to me, except, of course, when a long railway journey intervened;—and, sometimes, as an unexpected gladness, [my husband] would post two in one day, that I might be comforted concerning him.

On an important tour, like the one recorded [here], the letters would be illustrated by many amusing pen-and-ink sketches, of people, costumes, landscapes, trees, wells, or anything which particularly struck him.

Plans of the rooms he occupied in the various hotels were very frequent, and enabled me better to imagine the comfort, or otherwise, of his surroundings.

At one house at Nice, there was a delightful little platform or terrace opening out of his bedroom, and of this he sent a most elaborate sketch, so that I might share his pleasure in such an unusual addition to a sleeping apartment.'

'I am like Peter on the housetop,' he wrote, 'and though no sheet is let down to me, yet have I learned much that the sheet taught the apostle, and I count nothing common or unclean, no view unhallowed, no scenery to be avoided lest it should turn me away from communion with God. He has sanctified sea and mountain, housetop and street to me; and when my heart is devout—all these are helps, and not hindrances—to fellowship with Himself. I can little sympathize with those ultra-spiritually-minded people, who are so unspiritual that only the closed eye can enable them to think of their God.'

Susannah then added—

'I have said that the letters were 'illustrated,' but I think illuminated would be a better word … for, looking at them after these many years, with overflowing eyes, the little sketches seem to bear a rainbow light within them, and to sparkle with colours which only a devoted love could have blended. They remind me of the patient care bestowed upon the Psalters and Missals of the Middle Ages, when the hand of some pious man toiled day after day to decorate the vellum pages,—simply to prove the love of his heart, and witness to the truth of his devotion. My [husband] must have entertained some such feeling; for, at the end of a series of droll representations of women's head-gear which he had noticed in the streets of Botzen, he thus writes'—

'Now, sweetheart, may these trifles amuse you; I count it a holy work to draw them, if they cause you but one happy smile.'

Susannah then added—

'That I smiled on them then, and weep over them now, is but a natural consequence of the more complete separation which God has willed for us,—[Charles] dwelling in the land of glory—I, still tarrying amid the shadows of earth—but I verily believe that, when I join him … there will be tender remembrances of all these details of earthly love …

Surely we shall talk of all these things, in the pauses of adoring worship and of joyful service. There must be sweet converse in Heaven between those who loved, and suffered, and served together here below …

[The following passages give] extracts from the daily letters of my husband during his holiday journey to Rome, Naples, and Pompeii.

I have given them verbatim, only withholding allusions to domestic concerns and personal matters: and condensing, to a minimum, the sweet love-talk which in great measure helped me to bear the pain of these separations.

I have almost grudged to do this … for they shed so lovely a light upon his character …

Every here and there, I have allowed a sentence or two to reveal a glimpse of his great, tender, and true heart, as nothing else could have done; but the rest I have locked up again in the secret chambers of my memory.

The letters themselves are not set forth as examples of elegant style, or well-rounded periods, or even of graceful phraseology; they are simply a loving husband's daily notes to his sick wife—a record of his journeyings—

gladly and faithfully persevered in, with the sole object of pleasing her, and relieving her ... loneliness.

I hope they may interest many, and even instruct some.

Recent tourists in Italy's classic clime will be pleasantly reminded of their own travels, and be able to trace the progress that has been made during the past twenty-five years in the great work of excavating old Rome, and the buried cities on the Mediterranean shore ...

All who read [the letters] will, I trust, feel they are worthily enshrined in these pages.

❧ TRAVEL LETTERS ❧
(Summer 1871)

Our party met punctually at Victoria, and our journey to Dover consisted of parentheses of sunshine and paragraphs of mist. The woods look as if they were expiring amid the tears of nature. The sea was not like either sort of the prophet's figs, but was inclined to be irritable, without having vigour enough to work itself into actual passion.

The White Cliffs of Dover, from *Black's Guide to Kent* (1879).

Many suffered much from the marine malady [sea-sickness]; and, though we escaped it, yet we were glad to be again on the land, which was meant for man; the sea is evidently only designed for fishes and sailors.

We were asked our names at Calais; and, having answered to that first question of the Catechism, we were allowed to tread the soil of Republican France. We were soon satisfactorily 'restaurated', [restored,] and en route for Brussels, via Lille, Tournay, etc.

The whole land is like a neatly-kept garden, from which the tillers derive all the produce possible. We had a good journey, reached our hotel at six o'clock, dined, then walked down to the Arcade, which you will remember, and are now in our rooms, cosy and comfortable. The weather is delicious;—bright, clear, and balmy;—no fires needed; in fact, I am too warmly clad. The atmosphere is dry and light, and gives me new life.

The Port of Calais (published by Lemercier, circa 1860).

It seems very selfish to be writing thus to my dear prisoner at home, yet she loves me so much that the surest way to make her happy is to prove that I am enjoying my holiday.

All my love I send thee; may the everlasting arms encompass thee, even the arms of my God and thine!

഻ഺഺഺ

We were up early, and walked to the Botanical Gardens, and then on to the Church of St. Gudule, with its wonderful painted windows, some of them most ancient, others modern, but exquisite ...

We then drove to the Musee Wiertz, which I have before described to you.

It is certainly a very wonderful display of one man's powers, and a singular combination of the playful and the terrible. We saw all, and then went to the Luxembourg Station to continue our journey, by Waterloo, to Namur.

O 'days of auld lang syne,' how ye flashed before me, especially when we rode along by the Meuse and Huy to Liege, and thence to Chaudfontaine, Verviers, and Aix-la-Chapelle!

Alas! my dearest bides at home; and I, like a lone knight, can but remember the ladye of my love, for she rides not at my side as aforetime! The journey was exquisite for weather, temperature, and scenery; but it was long, and we were very hungry; so, when we sat down to table at 7:30, it was with the serious resolution to be avenged for our long fast.

This morning, I was up at six o'clock, revising a sermon. It is now raining for the first time since we left home; and this is convenient, for it makes it easier to remain indoors at work. Thus far, all has gone well, and we are grateful …

St. Martin's Church, Liege, from *Belgium and Nassau*, OR, *The Continental Tourist* (1838).

৯৵৵৸

It rained till we left Cologne yesterday, when we travelled to Mayence along the banks of the Rhine. The light was gone by 5:30, so that we saw nothing beyond Andernach; the sky was leaden, and the atmosphere hazy.

The woods, however, were ablaze with autumn fires, and the tints were inexpressibly lovely;—alas! the loveliness of decay. We reached here at 8:30, had tea, then crossed the bridge of boats, and returning, went up into the skies to bed [owing to the height of the hotel].

Munich.—Yesterday, we were on the railroad all day long.

We left Mayence at 10:20, and did not reach this city till 9:30.

The first part of the road was tame, then followed a chapter of forests with their matchless pomp of autumnal glory.

Anon, we mounted uphill into glens and mountain-valleys, which were presently succeeded by a river, with towns growing like osiers on its banks. This must be a superb city, and I want to spend to-day in seeing it; but we are in a fix. The only train over the Brenner leaves here at eleven at night. Innsbruck is the town at the foot of the pass on this side, and the train reaches and leaves there at three o'clock in the morning.

So, you see, if we go on a bit, we shall be no better off. To think of going over a pass in the dark, seems to me to be a wilful blasphemy of nature, if not of nature's God!

The Brenner Pass in 1873, from Stieler's *Italien* (1876).

We must find out if it cannot be managed otherwise than as a deed of darkness. We must have a carriage, if possible; and see the marvels of the mountains.

ৡৢৡৢ

[I find Munich] is an artistic city in all ways, a certain Greek-art appearance strikes one everywhere; not a sham, but a real reproduction of antiquity. We have been to the Glyptothek, a fine museum of statuary; but, really, after one has seen a few thousand nude figures, one feels content without any more anatomical models in stone.

Thence, we visited a large picture-gallery,—which I think almost equal to the Louvre,—full of masterpieces of most of the ancient schools.

We have been into a marvellous basilica, with pillars of the richest marble, and a ceiling of golden mosaic; also to the cathedral, to see the tomb of a German Emperor, a boy of the olden time, who has a bronze memorial of the noblest fashion.

Then we entered the studio of a renowned sculptor, and saw the plaster casts, the stone being chiselled, and the finished statues,—very interesting this. There is enough left for two or three days' enjoyment, but we must leave it; and I scarcely regret this, for the weather is very damp and depressing.

After all enquiries, I find we are compelled to go to-night at 11 o'clock, and pursue our weary way over the pass in the dark. Horses would require two days, and the roads are said to be in bad condition. 'What can't be cured, must be endured;' so I say, 'Southward Ho! at any price.' My heart flies to my wifey; I have just kissed my hand to her.

God bless her! Loads of love I telegraph by the soul-wire.

ço·ಶ/ಶ/ço

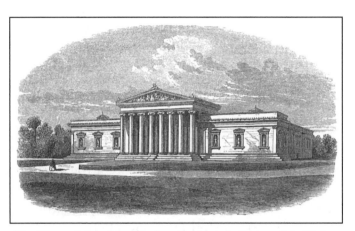

The Glyptothek in Munich, from Fergusson's *History of the Modern Styles of Architecture* (1862).

The Brenner is passed. We had some very uncomfortable experiences; the first part of the way, the guard wanted a coupon from us about every hour, and at Kuffstein we were hauled out of our nest, marched into the Austrian custom-house, made to wait, shivering, about thirty minutes, and then packed into a poor seedy carriage, cold and miserable, to continue our journey. Botzen was reached at last, but we were all so weary that we were glad to go into our rooms to rest till dinner.

Since then, we have walked round the old-fashioned town, and under its long-arched lines of shops. We have also heard service in the cathedral opposite to our hotel;

and very fine was the music, and very quaint the sight of a great crowd in the dark, except where a few had candles to see to read their mass-books.

Do you remember this old inn [Kaiser Krone], where Emperors and Popes have lodged? It is a singular building; our rooms are on the same floor as the *salle*, but we have to go up, and then down to them. I am weary, and am looking forward to to-morrow's rest.

ﻮﻫﻮﻫﻮ

Sabbath eve.—This has been a very gracious, happy, restful day. Did I but know that you are better, I don't think I should have more to wish, except your company.

We had a delicious morning service together;—read Psalm 22, and sang, 'Come, Let Us Sing The Song Of Songs,' and 'Where God Doth Dwell.' It was indeed a season of refreshing.

Then we saw a service at the cathedral. Large and devout congregations assemble here at each hour from 5 a.m. to 5 p.m. I have never seen any Romish place so well attended. Every person in the town seemed to go to one of the hourly services, and very attentive and earnest they appeared to be. We looked in several times, and twice heard a kind of litany, in German, by the whole congregation, led by a layman in common dress.

It reminded me of a prayer-meeting after service, for mass was over, and the altar-lights were put out, and then prayer broke out among all the people.

After dinner, we walked up a mountain's side in the bright sun's genial warmth, and what a view we had! Snowy Alps, and dark forests; and then, lower down, the meadows and the terraced vines, and lower yet, the plain of the Adige and its villages.

Our path led us by a series of shrines, similar to those at Varallo, but smaller, and at the end of the path was a 'Calvary.'

We had sweet communion together here, and great enjoyment of God's presence.

I am so much better in mind; I feel more elastic, light, and clear of forebodings. I now expect good news from my darling, whereas before I have felt sure of gloomy tidings.

A view in the Tyrol, along the Adige, from an engraving by Middiman (1819).

જ્જ્જ્જ્

Hotel Barbesi, Venice.—God be thanked for even the twinkling stars of better news in the letter I have just received from your dear self! It has poured with rain all day; indeed, they say it has rained for three whole weeks in these parts.

We left Botzen at six o'clock, driving through mist, cloud, and deluges above, and through wide, far-reaching floods upon either side. We only stayed two hours at Verona, but I had the joy of receiving your letter there.

On to Venice, found it better, but still very bad and wet. Had a gondola.

Our rooms are very good, but an evil smell pervades the place; whether it is the canals in general, or these rooms in particular, we cannot tell. A waiter, who has just come up, says it is the *tapis*, which is new; this is possible, but the nuisance is none the better for that.

The Grand Canal, Venice, an engraving after J.M.W. Turner, engraved by R. Brandard (1878).

Alas! the rain changes all things, and Venice looks sad in her sodden state.

We must hope for improvement.

After a splendid night's rest, I awoke at six o'clock, full of good spirits, and revised a sermon. After breakfast, we had a gondola, and went along the Grand Canal.

Glorious! About eleven, the tide turned, and rain began again, so we went to St Mark's, and saw the grand old cathedral, which is the same as ever, but needs sunshine to perfect it. Thence to the Doge's Palace,—you know all the details of these places.

The rain poured down when we got under the black cover of the gondola; but it was a delightful experience to be so sheltered, and yet to be moving through the floods.

We went to the Jesuits' Church, that fine marble one in the poorer part of the city;—you remember the curtains and carpet all reproduced in marble. Then we explored a glass manufactory, this was very interesting; they make mosaics, and mirrors, and chandeliers of the fine Venice glass, very wonderful to look upon.

Still it rained, and the water was over St. Mark's Square in front of the cathedral. Nevertheless, we visited Santa Maria Gloriosa, where is Canova's pyramidical tomb, and marble enough to stock a city; and then to Santa Maria del Salute, opposite to our hotel.

I have seen all these before, yet was still very much interested.

It is pitiable to see the poor people look soaked and only half-alive. Only the pigeons of St. Mark's are [happy]; they fly as a cloud, and swarm on the windows, and even enter the rooms of the houses all round the square; one might almost tread on them, they are so tame.

The unhappy vendors of shells and miniature gondolas will, I fear, be half-starved, and the flower-girls look very downhearted. The water now is over the paths, and up to the doors; yet Venice is not a bad place in wet weather, since you can keep dry in your gondola, and can look out through the windows.

St. Mark's Square, as it looked when Spurgeon saw it, from his *Autobiography*, vol. 3 (1899).

6 a.m.—I awake grateful for another night's peaceful rest, only to find myself very badly bitten by mosquitoes. A mosquito is the most terrible of beasts. A lion delights in blood, but he does not suck it from living animals; he does not carefully prolong their tortures. A viper poisons, but he is generally content with one use of his fangs; but these small-winged serpents bite in scores of places in succession.

My hands are a series of burning mountains. The creatures are as nearly omnipresent as Satan, which means that, though a mosquito cannot be everywhere, yet no mortal can be sure that he is not near him, or tell where he is not.

Curtains are a delusion, pastilles are a snare; the little enemies are irritated by such attempts to escape their malice, and give you double punishment.

O Italy! I have shed my blood for thy sake, and feel a love of thee (or something else) burning in my veins! The sooner I am away from thee, O fair Venice, the better, for thou dost deluge me by day, and devour me by night!

I wonder how my two companions have fared; I shall go, by-and-by, and look for their remains! I have opened my windows, and the pests are pouring in, eager and hungry; but, as I am up and dressed, there will be no more of me available for them at present.

A Gondola by the Ponte Rialto, Venice, Carlo Naya photo (1882).

To-day has been charming, and we have been in the gondola most of its lovely hours. The sights we saw were nothing compared with the delicious rowing in the city itself. Could you but have been there, it would have been as much of Paradise as this earth can ever yield.

Venice decays, but her autumn is fair. The fear is, lest the 'restorers' should come and deface her. We went to the Arsenal, but models of ships and guns would not interest you. Then to the Greek Church, and the Carmelites', and the Academy of Arts;—saw hosts of Madonnas and St. Sebastians, I am quite weary of them.

The outside of Venice is the treat, the beauty, the enjoyment.

We are off to-morrow very early for Florence; the air is loaded with mosquitoes, and my hands are 'a mask of sores,' as Mrs. Gamp would say, and both Mr. Passmore and I suffer much. Venice cannot be endured with these torments.

৵৵৵৵৵

We left Venice at 7:50, and proceeded to Bologna, which was reached by 12:10, after an uninteresting ride among perpetual trees festooned with vines,—muddy earth,—flooded fields,—and disconsolate maize-stalks.

From 1:20 to 5 o'clock, we were traversing the mountains between Bologna and Pistoia, and a more marvellous road it has never been my lot to see.

It was up, up, up, by the side of a torrent, which the rail crossed and recrossed, with rugged scenery of a

An engraving of the Arno River in Italy, and Pisa (1836).

sublime character on either hand. Then, in commencing the descent, we saw Pistoia, and the great plain of the Arno far below, like a raised map.

It was a truly wonderful view, but was soon gone; and we rushed down zigzags, and saw it again, and lost it every few minutes. It is almost miraculous that a train can keep to the rails upon such descents. Down below at Pistoia, we found that the floods had done great damage; but the railway was all right, so we reached Florence about seven o'clock.

All this is very uninteresting to read, but it was pleasant to experience, while good companionship and the sunshine made the whole journey enjoyable.

Though wearied by the long hours of travelling, I am in every way more fresh and free from depression. May the

Lord enrich me also in spiritual blessings, and send me back more capable of serving Him than I have ever been!

We are off early to-morrow, so now, my darling, may God watch over thee, bless thee, and keep thee, and restore me to thee in joy and peace!

Oceans of love, and as many kisses for you as the sand on the sea-shore.

My next letter will be from 'the city of the seven hills,' if all is well.

We are in Rome. Let a man say what he will, there is a thrill passes through his soul, at the thought of being in Rome, that he cannot experience anywhere else, except in the city of our Lord,—Jerusalem. There are interests and associations that cluster about 'the eternal city' that a man must feel, if he has any soul at all.

Rome, City of the Seven Hills, from the
Autobiography, vol. 3 (1899).

You remember that, last year, we started off for our first day's sight-seeing without a guide, and wandered about without knowing whither we went; this time, I can act as guide and interpreter, and am able to observe much which, on a former occasion, I had not noticed. To-day, we went down the Corso, and up the Capitol. There are new excavations at its foot. We passed down the other side to the Forum, where they are still digging.

Rome of the olden time is buried beneath itself, under its own ruins, and the Forum lies some ten, fifteen, and in some places thirty feet of earth below the present level.

I soon found myself on what I knew to be the Via Sacra, along which the triumphal processions passed when the great generals returned from war, and climbed the Capitol in state; and it was a memorable thing to stand before the Arch of Titus, and gaze upon its bas-reliefs. There is Titus returning from the siege of Jerusalem, with the seven-branched golden candlestick, and the silver trumpets; and, while these things stand there, it is idle for infidels to say that the Bible is not true. It is good history.

Nobody doubts what is written in stone upon the Arch of Titus, but the same story is found in the Book; and the more discoveries that are made of ancient cities, especially in Palestine, the more will the truth of the Book be confirmed, and the record upon stone will be found to tally with what is written on the tablets of God's Word.

Then we came to the Colosseum. What a place it is! Two-thirds of it are gone, and yet enough remains wherewith to build a great city! I climbed to the very top.

The Colosseum, as Spurgeon saw it, from the
Autobiography, vol. 3 (1899).

Under an arch of one of the great corridors we sat down,
and sang, 'Am I A Soldier Of The Cross?' 'I'm Not
Ashamed To Own My Lord,' and 'Jesu's Tremendous
Name;' and then I preached a little sermon from the text,
'Come, behold the works of the Lord, what desolations
He hath made in the earth;' then we prayed, and sang…

> Ashamed of Jesus? Sooner far
> Let evening blush to own a star.
> He sheds the beams of light divine
> O'er this benighted soul of mine.

Just then, two persons went by, and said, in broad
American, 'Don't let us disturb you.' To which
I answered, 'Come and join,' but they replied, 'Our
time is too short,' so we sang the Doxology, and went

on. Pretty bold this, in such a public place, but very sweet to be remembered. 'Boylston' rolled along the vaulted tunnels like a battle-song.

The Baths of Titus, from *Li monumenti più celebri di Roma antica* (1850).

We went down to the Appian Way, and on to the baths of Titus.

By a mistake, I took the party up a lane, and through the wrong gate; but, after all, this was fortunate, for it brought us to the top of the immense structure; and, looking down, we saw the rooms which before I had only seen from below, and this view gave us a better idea of their vastness and mystery. The building is a huge ruin, built upon a ruin. Nero had a golden palace here, but when Titus came into power, he buried it.

Its roof was made of great arches, massive and strong, so he bored holes through them, and poured in rubbish till the place was filled up, and then he built his baths on the top of all. His work is ruined; but now, part of the palace below has been dug out, and they have found gems of art, enough to fill hundreds of museums.

Getting to the right entrance, we came across the custodian, an old, wounded soldier, who showed us over the whole place, as far as practicable, telling us all he knew, pointing out every fresco, and putting a delightful zest into it for us all.

It is a place of marvels! Its passages and rooms are countless, vast, weird, and most impressive; one could spend a week there, and then begin again. The excavations have brought to light treasures of porphyry, marble, and statues; and the paintings and frescoes of eighteen hundred years ago are as fresh as if they were painted yesterday. Your guide has a long pole, into which he screws another long pole with a lighted candle at the end, this he holds up as high as possible, and you see the paintings on the roof of Nero's palace.

There are said to be two hundred rooms still unexcavated, and no one knows what treasures of art they may conceal.

Strange to say, there is yet another house beneath this golden palace, for Nero built over the house of Mecaenas, the friend of Horace; and, after digging deep down, they have come to the mosaic pavements of the first structure erected on this extraordinary spot. I want a bigger head, to take all these wonders in, and hold my thoughts!

Ruins of the Palace of the Caesars on the Palatine Hill, by
James Hakewill (1817).

After all this, we went a little further, to the Palace of
the Caesars, which is a mile and a-half round, and is
being excavated.

All is ruined, but it is so far opened up as to show
the lower rooms, and the first, or Imperial floor.
It consisted of many palaces, and would take a month
to explore.

In one part, I saw rooms just dug out, as fresh as when
originally decorated, and remarkably like the Pompeian
house in the Crystal Palace.

There was Caesar's great hall, the place of his
throne, the bath of the harem, the library, the academy

or residence for philosophers, and the rooms for the Pretorian guard.

In fact, the whole Palatine Hill is a palace; and as they dig down, they come to vast chambers and corridors which seem endless. One of these, quite as long as our Nightingale Lane, has its mosaic pavement all complete; we looked down from a great height upon it, and there were opened places far below that.

The walls are usually seven to ten feet thick, so the work must be very heavy. I should think all kinds of marble in the world can be picked up here; it is just a vast quarry! What heaps of broken wine-jars,—the champagne bottles of the Caesars!

It is a mountain of ruins of porphyry, alabaster, and all precious things! From its top you see other great ruins of temples, basilicas, palaces, and theatres!

తింతింతింతిం

Then the guide said, 'Now you must come and see the baths of Caracalla.'

I was bewildered, lost, confounded; but I went, and found a building more than a mile in length, which beat all we had seen before, and made me feel as if my senses would give way. These enormous baths could accommodate 1,600 persons at a time; they were in tiers, one for men, another for women, the third for slaves.

There were hot baths, cold baths, steam baths, swimming baths; and all these were floored with mosaics which we saw uncovered as we stood there.

The roof was destroyed by the Goths; and when it fell in, it smashed the floor; but here and there great portions—as big as our lawn—are left intact, and one could see the lovely patterns of the mosaic,—each room different. The huge brick walls still stand, but the marble facing is almost all gone.

I think no living man can conceive what the place must have been in its glory. I needed to go to bed, to sleep off my stupor of wonder! I am foolish to try to write about it.

It is like a tadpole describing a sea! The Farnese family have taken the fine statues and other treasures to Naples; but there are acres yet to be dug out, in which, doubtless, many more are buried, but it is too great an expense to dig away very fast.

I had one delicious half-hour during the day. I sat down alone opposite to St. Peter's, and felt as if in Elysium. The snow gone, the sun shining, and on the

St. Peter's Basilica, from the *Autobiography*, vol. 3 (1899).

great obelisk I saw words which cheered my soul; they were these, 'Christ conquers, Christ reigns, Christ rules, Christ defends His people from all evil.'

The Lord be praised; this is true, and the Pope and all the world shall know it! I love my love amidst all these great thoughts. She is my palace, my throne, my empress, my Rome, my world; yet I have more, my Saviour, my Heaven! Bless you, my own!

To-day is the Sabbath, and has been up till now most sweetly calm and happy.

We had our little service, with breaking of bread, and the Lord was with us. I read a sermon, and our song and prayer were 'in the Spirit.'

May it please the Lord of peace to give the like holy rest to my beloved! We then walked on the Pincian [Monte Pincio], where there are few people during the day, but lovely groves, and beds of roses, with seats in every corner, and all Rome at one's feet.

It was truly Sabbatic. All that nature and art can do, is to be seen in these gardens, where the loveliest statues look down upon you, and fountains ripple to tunes of peace, and aromatic trees breathe perfume. A statue of Jochebed laying Moses in his ark of bulrushes among the reeds, struck me as charming to the last degree. It stood as the centre of a fountain, reeds and water-lilies grew at the rocky base, and the ripples of the little hidden jets made wavelets round the ark.

Can you imagine it? Nothing in modern art has pleased me more,—perhaps nothing so much. This has been a blessed day to me, and I have been feeling

The view southwest from Monte Pincio to St Peter's, photo by Underwood & Underwood (circa. 1890).

so well; I almost tremble lest it should be too good to continue.

Another day of wonders! This morning, we drove to the great amphitheatre of Marcellus, which once held 20,000 persons, and is far older than the Colosseum.

It is buried for fourteen feet, and much built over and hidden; around it is a market for the poor, where I saw baskets full of cigar-ends which had no doubt been picked up in the street, and were being sold to be smoked in pipes.

What would Marcellus have thought of this? Then we saw the long covered way which led from the theatre to the baths of Agrippa,—a great colonnade, of which some pillars are visible, and others are built into the houses of the street which occupies its place. From thence to the Jews' quarter, where the same use of old stones is apparent; capitals, friezes, cornices, and all sorts of marbles are let into the walls of the dwellings.

Ah! the cruelties the Jews have suffered in that Ghetto, the barbarities which have there been inflicted upon God's ancient people!

Their district is often flooded by the Tiber; and, on one occasion, when they made an appeal to the papal authorities, because their houses were ten or twelve feet under water, the only answer they received was that the water would do the Jews good! ... Time would fail to tell of their sufferings and privations, besides which they were forced to pay large sums of money to their oppressors. Matters have mended somewhat lately, and they are relieved from many of the most cruel persecutions of former days; but they are oppressed still ...

৵৵৵৵

To-day we went several miles along the Appian Way. What bliss ever to see it!

On both sides, for many miles, it is skirted by tombs, temples, columbaria, and ruins of villas in continuous lines. It is a British Museum ten miles long!

I felt a strange joy in walking along the same road which Paul trod, when the brethren from Rome came to meet him. From it can be seen Tusculum and Tivoli, and the long line of the Claudian aqueduct, on arches all the way from the mountains into Rome, as also the temple of Romulus, and the great circus of Maxentius.

What a world of wonders! We went as far as the Casale Rotundo, a round tomb so large that, being full of rubbish, there is a house, and stables, and an olive garden on the top.

We wanted to investigate, so climbed up, and were rewarded by the sight of a family of very scantily-clothed children; their mother and an old woman were baking maize bread in a hole in the wall of the tomb. They had

Along the Appian Way, photo by Underwood & Underwood
(circa. 1890).

kneaded it in a wheelbarrow, and the children looked as if they needed it, too…

On our way back, when nearly as far as the old walls, we turned down a lane to visit the catacombs of Calixtus. Candles were provided, and we went down to the second tier; there are five of these, one below another. I do not know how far we went, but it seemed miles;—passages just wide enough for me to pass through, opening into rooms every now and then, and with many cross-roads where one could soon be lost.

Here were countless graves, here and there skeletons, emblems, places for lamps, frescoes of ancient date, and many interesting memorials.

It was a new scene to me, but deeply solemn and touching.

Think of it,—that this was only one set of chambers and passages, and that there was one above, and three deeper down!

There are from five to six graves, one above the other, in each passage, and the whole place is full right along. These tombs are open in most cases, for the doors or stones which closed them are taken away to museums. This is the best and most convenient catacomb for tourists to see; but there are, I believe, sixty others …

৵৵৵৵

Then we drove to St. John Lateran, 'the mother of all churches,' and I shall here only dare to write of one thing which, to my dying day, I shall never forget. I do not know that I ever felt my blood boil so with indignation or my heart melt so much with pity as when I saw the Santa Scala, down which our blessed Lord is said to have come from Pilate's hall.

It was a pitiable sight to see old people, grey headed men, young women, and little children with their mothers, crawling up and down this staircase on their knees, kissing the bottom step, and touching it with their forehead, and doing likewise to the middle and top steps, because they say our Saviour fainted at those places.

As I stood there, I could only pray that another Luther might arise, and thunder forth the fact that men are not justified by works, but by faith alone. It was an awful thought to me that all these poor creatures should believe that they gained a hundred days' indulgence and the pardon of their sins every time they crawled up that staircase, and that every step their knees kneeled on meant so many days less of purgatory for them.

The stairs are covered with wood, which has been three times renewed, having been worn away by the knees of the votaries! My heart feels all on a blaze with righteous anger.

O miserable world, thus to dishonour the ever-blessed Lamb! ...

৽৵৶৽

We went to St. Peter's to finish the day with music, and it was fine indeed; but I was jostled in a crowd of people so highly perfumed with garlic, that I soon made my escape to the outskirts to have another look round the great joss-house.

Here I learned some English history, for I saw Canova's tomb to the memory of James III, Charles III, and Henry IX, Kings of England! Ask the boys if they ever read of them.

They were the last of the Stuarts;—the Pretender,—his son, Charles Edward, or 'bonnie Prince Charlie,'—and his son.

What hundreds of other things I have seen this day, cannot now, and perhaps never will be told. I have stayed up late to put this down for fear of forgetting it, and also because it may be I shall have less time to-morrow when preparing to preach.

God bless thee, dearest, and be thou glad, with me, that no 'strong delusion to believe a lie' has fallen upon us. To-day has taught me a year's learning.

The Lord make it useful to His Church!

ง๏จจจจจจ

The Pope's Coachman, a postcard sent home by Spurgeon, from the *Autobiography*, vol. 3 (1899).

I send a picture of the Pope's coachman. What a swell he is!

[It] will make a sensation in the magic-lantern.

Yesterday morning, when I preached in the Presbyterian Chapel, all was quiet and delightful; but at night, in Rome, while my words were being translated by Mr. Wall, we were stopped by questioners. It was requested that they would reserve their enquiries till the end of the service, but the opponents were impatient. A paper was passed up from a Catholic lady, to say that a secular priest was present, a man of great ability, and a personal friend of the Pope, and that he was sent on purpose to discuss.

So, presently, a man of unprepossessing appearance began to assail us with arguments from a sceptical standpoint, upon which he received such an answer that he shifted his ground, and declared that none had any right to teach save 'the Church.'

Mr. Wall replied to this, and the man changed his tactics again.

Then, up rose a Waldensian minister, who spoke so well that the people broke out in cheers and clapping. This was suppressed, and again the enemy thundered forth his threats. He was answered by several, and told that he had shifted his ground, and was a priest; and Mr. Wall challenged him to a public dispute at any place he chose to name. This he declined, and seeing that the people grew warm, he wisely withdrew.

One word from us, and he would have been put out of the window.

The incident pleased Mr. Wall, for it created excitement, and will bring more to hear; but I was far from happy about it, and would gladly have been spared such a scene. Glory be to God, there is a living church in Rome, and the way in which they have gained converts has been by opposition; the notoriety which it has given them has brought many to hear the gospel. Bravely the work goes on, and the baptized lead the way.

The leaders are two good fellows, pronounced Baptists, believing firmly that their church is that of the catacombs, and the only true Church of Christ in Rome; the others, they say, are the churches of Luther, and Knox, and Wesley, and Waldo,—theirs is the only old original. I gently combat their restrictiveness, but do not wonder at it.

৵৽৵৽৵

We have been to another catacomb, one not often visited. It is named after St. Ponziano, and is situated outside Rome, in a vineyard, a good way from the walls, and though truly ancient, it is not very far opened up, but you have to go down very deep. A man, who calls himself 'the dove of the catacombs' (he must mean 'bat'), took us down.

We went a long, long way, each of us carrying a taper, and at last we came to a place where some eight roads meet underground. Seven of these were closed, but we found what we had specially come to see. This was a baptistery. It was full of sweet, clear, running water, about four feet deep, and above it was a painting in fresco of our Lord standing up to his waist in the water, and John putting his hand on the sacred head, that it, too, might be immersed;—he was not pouring the water on him. Here we stood, and prayed to the blessed One into whose Name we had been buried by baptism. It was a solemn moment.

Here also were two other frescoes of our Lord,—very beautiful faces; and the Alpha and Omega, and Christian monogram symbols, which are so plain and natural that they do not come under the head of superstition. There were, however, bones in plenty, and the place was very hot and close, so we were glad soon to escape into the open air ...

৩০৯৩৯

You would have liked to have been with us when we went to see the columbaria, near the St. Sebastian gate. We visited two of them; they are singular places, like vast dovecots, but they are not for doves. It is strange to look upon the spot where thousands upon thousands of Rome's wealthy citizens have for many ages lain in little heaps of ashes.

The bodies of the dead were burned, and the dust was preserved in small urns which were kept in these curious places. Some persons had a family columbarium; in other cases, companies were formed for their construction, and they were then let out in portions as required. The niches are like small, vaulted chambers, and there will be in them, sometimes an urn, sometimes a lamp, or a small

99

bust, while frequently the name and age of the deceased will be found on a slab of marble over the recess.

The St Sebastian Gate, Porta Appia, photo by
Underwood & Underwood (1900).

In each of these small spaces, there are two holes sunk to receive the ashes if an urn is not used, and these have lids to cover the remains. These great square buildings contained many hundreds of these 'nests' for the dead, and a visit to them leaves a strangely-solemn impression on the mind.

❧❧❧

I had two such precious letters from you this morning, worth to me far more than all the gems of ancient or modern art. The material of which they are composed is their main value, though there is also no mean skill revealed in its manipulation.

They are pure as alabaster, far more precious than porphyry or verd antique; no mention shall be made of malachite or onyx, for love surpasses them all.

We are off to Naples to-day.

A TRAVELLER'S LETTERS HOME
(continued)

This morning, we drove through Naples for, I should think, six or seven miles or more. It is a crowded city, full of stirs, full of business, and full of pleasure.

Horses seem innumerable, they are decorated profusely, and the carriages are very comfortable; but, I am sorry to say, the men drive furiously, and make me very nervous. Old women are numerous and hideous, beggars pestiferous, and dealers intensely persevering.

The Bay of Naples, and Mount Vesuvius, published by Fisher, Son & Co. of London (1846).

But what a bay! What a sea and climate! No one ought to be ill here.

We have been over the museum—full of frescoes from Pompeii, gleanings from the catacombs, pickings from the Appian Way, stealings from the baths of Caracalla and other places. Naples has taken away from Rome the best of the ancient statuary and treasures, and prepared a vast museum for the spoils. We saw thousands of precious things, enough for a year's inspection; but the Pompeian remains were the most important.

There were surgical instruments exactly like those of the present day;—cottage-loaves of bread, stewpans, colanders, ladles, and all cookery things just like our own. The safes for money were just like old plate-chests. There were cotton, silk, and thread, in skeins and hanks, and large knitting and netting needles. Indeed, the people then had all we have now; even earthen money-boxes with a slit in the top, such as the children have in our country villages. There were plenty of proofs that the people were sinners, and of a scarlet dye, too.

It was curious to see the colours in a painter's shop, the bottles and drugs of a chemist, and the tools of other traders. We saw also a splendid collection of ancient gems and cameos, most costly and lovely. I never saw so many gathered together before.

৵৵৵৵৵

We drove from the museum to the site of a new field of lava, which flowed down from Vesuvius last April. It is just beyond the houses of suburban Naples, and was very different from what I had expected. It had crossed our road, and passed on through a vineyard,—this was one tongue of the stream. Then we crossed a second by a road made near it, and came to a village through which the largest stream had burned its way.

It is a huge incandescent sea of the outflow of the volcano; men were blasting and using pickaxes to open up the road which the flood had completely blocked. We were soon upon the lava; it has a surface like a heap of ashes, supposing that every ash should weigh a ton or two. It is still hot, and in some places smoking. I should have investigated it carefully, and with interest, only a horde of children, beggars, and women with babies gave us no rest, but continued crying, and imploring alms, and offering us pieces picked out of the mass.

Much of the strange material is far too hot to hold, and our feet felt the heat as we walked across the surface. The stream has partly destroyed several houses, and cut the village in two; people are living in the half of a house which stands, the other half being burned and filled up with the molten substance.

Vesuvius, high above us, is only giving out a little smoke, and seems quiet enough. As I could never climb up to the crater, I think we shall be content to have seen this lava torrent.

ৡৄৢৣৡৣৢ

Our hotel here is vast and empty; we have excellent rooms, and are thoroughly comfortable. There is music continually, and very fair music, too, though not so sweet as silence. Everybody makes all the noise possible, and quiet dwells beyond the sea.

Rome is a sepulchre,—this city teems with life. You are not out of the door a moment before you are entreated to have a carriage, buy fruit, fish, pictures, papers, or something. The side-streets swarm with people, who appear to live in them …

It is like living in a museum; but as to the beauty and gracefulness of which we read so much, I cannot detect it, though really looking for it. Persons over forty look worn out, and females at that age are haggard; over that period, they are ghastly and mummified. Macaroni hangs out, in some quarters, before the doors on lines to dry; and the flies, which are numerous upon it, give it anything but an attractive appearance.

To-morrow, we hope to go to Pompeii.

I am now thinking about next month's [issue of *The Sword and the Trowel*] magazine, and devoutly wish I could light upon a subject for an article,—but my brain is dull.

৯৽৶৶

We have seen Pompeii. We drove there, and it took us three hours, almost all of it between long lines of houses, like one continuous street. At the town of Resina, we passed Herculaneum, but did not enter it, as Pompeii is more worth seeing. Then we went through a town which has, I think, been seven times destroyed by Vesuvius, and is now crowded with people. There we saw the lava by the side of, and under the houses, hard as a rock; and the roads are generally paved with great flags of the same material.

Though driving by the shore of the bay, we seldom saw the water, for even where there was no town, there were high walls, and, worst of all, off the stones the white dust was suffocating, and made us all look like millers. However, we reached Pompeii at last, and I can only say, in a sentence, it exceeds in interest all I have seen before, even in Rome.

Pompeii and Mount Vesuvius, photo by
Underwood & Underwood (1900).

I walked on, on, on, from twelve to four o'clock, lost in wonder amid the miles of streets of this buried city, now silent and open to the gazer's eye. To convey a worthy idea of it to you, would be impossible, even in a ream of paper.

We entered at the Street of Tombs, which was outside the gate. In it were houses, shops, taverns, a fountain, and several tombs.

The house of Diomed greatly interested us. We went upstairs and downstairs, and then into the cellars where were still the amphorae, or wine-bottles, leaning against the wall in rows, the pointed end being stuck into the ground, and the rows set together in dry dust, in exactly the same way as we place articles in sawdust. In the cellars were found eighteen skeletons of women who had fled there for shelter.

The House of Diomed, from Bulwer-Lytton's *The Last Days of Pompeii*, illustrated (circa. 1870).

The photograph I send shows the garden, with covered walk round it, and tank for live fish. In this street were several places for seats in the shade, made in great semicircles, so that a score of persons could rest at once. Near the gate was the niche where the soldier was found who kept his watch while others fled. We could not think of going up and down all the streets; it would need many days to see all.

The city was, I should think, a watering-place for the wealthy. No poor class of houses has yet been discovered. It was paved with great slabs of stone, which are worn deeply with cart or chariot wheels. Across the streets were huge stepping-stones, just wide enough to allow wheels to go on each side; but either they had no horses to the cars in these streets, or else they must have been trained to step over. In some places were horsing-blocks, in others there were holes in the kerbstone, to pass a rope through to tie up a horse.

The houses are many of them palaces, and contained great treasures of art, which are now in museums, but enough is left in each case to show what they were. Frescoes remain in abundance, and grottoes, and garden fountains, and marble terraces for cascades of water.

It is a world of wonders.

৩৯৯৯৯

In one part of the city, a noble owner had let the corner of his house to a vendor of warm wines, and there is his marble counter, with the holes therein for his warming-pots. Stains of wine were on the counter when it was first uncovered.

We saw the back parlour of a drinking-shop, with pictures on the wall of a decidedly non-teetotal character. There were several bakers' shops with hand-mills, the tops of which turned round on a stone, and ground well, no doubt. In one, we saw the oven, with a water-jar near it,—in this place were found 183 loaves of bread.

In the doctors' and chemists' shops, when opened, they saw the medicines as they were when entombed, and even pills left in the process of rolling! In the custom-house were standard weights and measures. Soap factories have their evaporating-pans remaining.

Oil vessels abound; and in one, made of glass, some of the oil may still be seen. Cookshops had in them all the stewpans, gridirons, and other necessities of the trade.

We saw jewellers' shops, artists' studios, and streets of grocers' and drapers' shops, many with signs over their doors.

৯৹৵৵৵৹

The baths impressed me much, for they had been newly built when the awful tragedy took place, and look as if they were opened yesterday;—a fine cold plunge-bath, with water carried high for a 'shower', a dressing-room with niches for brushes, combs, and pomades,—all of which were there, but have been removed to museums;—and a great brazier in green bronze, with seats round it for the bathers to dry themselves;—a warm bath, and a vapour bath all perfect, and looking ready for use to-morrow.

The Forum was vast, and had in it the facades of several magnificent temples, the remains of which reveal their former glory. The pedestals of the statues of the eminent men of the town remain with their names upon them.

We saw the tragic and comic theatres, and the amphitheatre which held 20,000 persons, in which the people were assembled when the eruption came, and from which they escaped, but had to flee to the fields, and leave their houses for ever.

The Amphitheatre at Pompeii (1870 photo).

In the Temple of Isis, we saw the places where the priests were concealed when they made the goddess deliver her oracles! We saw the lady herself in the museum, with a pipe at the back of her head, which was fixed in the wall, and served as the secret speaking-tube. The priests of Isis were found dead at her shrine; one of them with an axe had cut through two walls to get out, but had not succeeded. Poor creature!

In a money-changer's house, we saw his skeleton, lying on its face, with outstretched arms and hands; much money was found near him. In the barracks were sixty-three persons, soldiers' and officers' wives. Here were the stocks which had been used for the punishment of refractory soldiers.

In the Street of Mercury is a triumphal arch, on which stood a statue of Nero, found nearly perfect. Here, too, we noted a drinking-fountain, and a house with its exterior richly adorned with red frescoes. In a vast Hall of Justice were cells under the magistrates' bench; and in these, three prisoners were found …

࣭࣭ஒ࣭ஒ࣭ஒ

We saw the digging still going on, and the mounds of removed rubbish were like high railway embankments. No roofs remain, but spouts for the rain-water are there in great abundance; they are in the form of dogs' and lions' heads and other quaint devices. No stables have yet been uncovered, but the carts, which stood at the inn doors, have left their iron tires, the skeletons of the horses, and their bits, to bear witness to their former existence.

Skeletons of dogs and cats were there, and in a pan was a sucking pig prepared and just ready for roasting! I saw also a pot on a tripod, or trivet, which, when discovered, actually had water in it! I feel ashamed to write so badly on such a theme, but I cannot do better. It is too vast a task for me, and I fail to recollect a tithe of it. I must cease writing to-night, but I continue to breathe loving assurances to my sweet wifey.

৵৵৵৵৵

We have been in a steamer to the Island of Capri, calling at Sorrento on the way;—a glorious excursion, but we failed in our great object, which was, to see the Blue Grotto.

The sea was too rough to permit entrance, as the opening is only three feet high, and no one can get in except during smooth water, and when the wind is from a certain quarter. However, we stayed a couple of hours on the island, which is precipitous, so I did not climb, but sat on a balcony, enjoying the marvellous scene.

We reached Naples late, for the boat was slow; but first the sunset, and then the moonlight, gave us two charming effects, to which Vesuvius added by smoking almost continuously. This little trip served as a pleasant rest and refreshment after the toil and the dust of Pompeii.

৵৵৵৵৵

To-day, we have had a long and splendid drive to the other side of the bay. First along the quay, then through a tunnel almost half a mile long, and then skirting the bay, by road to Puteoli, where Paul landed;—we saw the spot (as is supposed), and the commencement of the Appian Way which he followed till he reached Rome.

At Puteoli, we first went into the crater of the Solfatara, a semi-extinct volcano, which has not been in eruption since 1198, when it destroyed ancient Puteoli.

It is grown over with shrubs and small trees. A man throws down a big stone, which makes it all sound, and shows you that the whole vast area is hollow. You are led to a great hole in the side of the hill, whence pours out, with the roar of an engine blowing off steam, a great quantity of sulphureous vapour.

All around is brimstone, and with a long kind of hoe a man rakes out bits from the mouth of the huge oven. The ground is very hot, and an odour, which is anything but dainty, prevails. You can go right up to it with perfect ease and safety. The vapour is said to cure gout, but one must stand in it some time every day for a month!

When Vesuvius is furious, Solfatara subsides, so there seems good evidence that the two, though twelve miles apart, are vents of the same fires.

We looked down on the Temple of Serapis; it has been up and down, and in and out of the sea several times, as the restless coast has risen or fallen. It is now out of water, but is remarkable rather for its history than for its present beauty.

৯৵৵৵৵

We drove on by the crater of Monte Barbaro and that of Monte Nuovo.

This last volcano sprang up in a night in 1538, covered a village, stopped a great canal, and did no end of mischief; but since then it has been quiet, and allowed itself to furnish soil enough for brushwood, which makes it look like a green pyramid.

On the other side of this hill is the famous lake of Avernus, of which Virgil wrote, and by the side of which he placed the entrance to Hades. The dense woods which smothered it have been cut down, and it has by no means a repulsive appearance now; but it is a channel for the escape of noxious gases, and is, no doubt, the crater of a volcano.

We did not enter the Sybil's Cave, or otherwise enquire of Pluto and Proserpine; but drove on, through the ruined city of Cumae, to the lake of Fusaro or

Lake Avernus, as shown in the book *Italian Scenery* (1817).

Acheron, another circular basin. Here oysters were cultivated till the lake gave out mephitic vapours, and killed the bivalves. The water has become pure again, and the industry has recommenced.

Passing by Virgil's Elysian fields, and manifold wonders, we came to Misenum, and the village of Bacoli. Here we left the carriage, and ascended the hill to see what is called the Piscina Mirabilis,—a vast underground reservoir, which once contained water brought by the Julian aqueduct from some fifty miles' distance.

It is dry now, and we descended a long flight of steps to the bottom. It has a roof supported by forty-eight huge columns; it is 220 feet long, and 82 feet broad. There are traces of water having filled it up to the spring of the arches, and the place where the water entered is very plainly to be seen. There are great openings in the roof, down which hang festoons of creeping plants. The place was very chilly, and coming up forty steps out of it seemed like leaving a sepulchre. Yet it was a sight to be remembered to one's dying day …

We went into Baiae, and entered a queer little osieria, or inn, and had some poor would-be oysters, bread and butter, and green lemons, freshly gathered from the tree. The view was glorious indeed, nothing could excel it; great ruined temples and villas were everywhere, and made a picture of exceeding beauty.

෨෬෬෨

The drive home was by the sea, and we could perceive buildings down at the bottom, under the clear blue water.

These have been brought down by the depression of the land upon which they stood, owing to earthquakes. We crossed a lava torrent which had come from Monte Nuova, and then we went on by our former road through Puteoli, till we left it to return to Naples without traversing the tunnel. This road took us up on one side of the promontory of Posilippo, whence we saw Ischia, Puteoli, Baia:, and Misenum; and then we went down the other side, with Capri, Sorrento, Vesuvius, and Naples, all in full view.

We were quickly down among the grand equipages which fill the Riviera di Chiaia; and, dashing along as fast as any of them, we were soon at the hotel door; and, since table d'hote, I have been writing this long narration for you.

The air here is balmy, the atmosphere dry, the heat great in the sun, but bearable in the shade. Mosquitoes are fewer and less voracious than in Venice. Everything is restorative to the system, and exhilarating ...

To-morrow will be the Sabbath, and in this I rejoice, for rest is sweet, and sweetest when made 'holiness to the Lord.' I send tons of love to you, hot as fresh lava.

God bless you with His best blessings!

∽∾∾∽

It is the Sabbath, quiet and restful.

We have had a delightful service, and I have written for my note-book and the Magazine; so there will be a little less for my dear one, but there is nothing new to tell.

I have been so grandly well all this time that I do not know how to be grateful enough, and my heart is light because you are better; my soul is at rest, my spirit leaps. I am indeed a debtor to Him who restoreth my soul. Blessed be His holy Name for ever and ever! We are very quiet, for there are no other visitors in the house; we have the best rooms, nice beds, well-curtained from mosquitoes. There is a house between us and the sea, but we can see the bay on each side of it, and Vesuvius if we go out on the balcony.

The climate is like Heaven below, and cannot but be a medicine to the sick.

I send you a photograph of a slave who was found in Pompeii close behind his master, and carrying a bag of money, both of them endeavouring to escape. It is a perfect model, covered with incrustations.

I have also sent the photograph of a grotto, or rather, ancient fountain in mosaic, which is in one of the houses. They used to put a lamp inside the grotesque heads. Water fell in a little cascade down the steps. It seems in odd taste, but there are several such in the gardens of the buried villas.

To-morrow we hope to be travelling.

God be with thee, mine own, and give thee peace and healing! My heart is everywhere and ever thine.

Again in Rome. Waking somewhat early this morning, I have risen to write to mine own darling wife. The fact is, I am afraid there will be a gap in the correspondence, and I shall be very sorry if it turns out to be so. Just as we left Naples, the rain began to descend, the warmth was gone, and we had a cool, if not a cold journey here. The fall in the temperature seemed to affect me, and I had a very disturbed and uncomfortable night.

I am, however, so grateful for my long spell of rest, night by night, that this does not depress me, although I hoped that I was getting beyond the reach of such restless hours.

Yesterday was wet every now and then, but I had to devote the day to the [next issue of *The Sword and the Trowel*] magazine, and therefore it mattered not. I stole out to the Pantheon, and the Lateran, and then in again.

Not being in harness, I worked slowly, and the matter came not until the mind had been much squeezed. How much more pleasant is the outbursting juice of the grape

A view of the Pantheon, Rome, by Giuseppe Acquaroni (1810).

when it yields its streams to the lightest pressure of the vintner's hand!

Yet duty had to be done, and I did it; but have more yet to do.

Three dear letters awaited me here. 'Not worth sixpence,' did you say ? They are worth a mint to me; they are mosaics of which every little bit is a gem. Naples has been a great treat; how I wish you could have been there, but I should not like you to see how horses are treated, it would make you quite unhappy. The Neapolitans load up their carriages most cruelly. I never saw so many horses, mules, and donkeys in my life before in proportion to the people.

Everybody drives or rides, and they are all in a great hurry, too.

Now, my wifey, this brings great galleons of love to you, and a cargo of kisses lies under the hatches. Just pull them up, and let the creatures fly in the air; innumerable they will be as the clouds of doves which flew over the olive gardens of Judaea in the olden time, and every one has its own tender voice ...

৬৩৵৶৵৶

Florence.—By an unfortunate mistake as to train, we were prevented from leaving Rome early this morning, so we have done a little more sight-seeing. One of our party is of the Mark Tapley school, and always persuades us that any hitch in our plans is a capital thing, and could not have happened better. We went off to Santa Maria Maggiore, and there saw the various chapels, and precious stones, and rare marbles, and bronzes, etc., etc.

The old verger was so eloquent in Italian that I made out nearly all he said. Then we went to the Borghese Palace, and saw long rooms of pictures, mostly saints and virgins. In these rooms were two sweet little fountains of water, and glasses for the visitors to drink from. This is a private palace, but the public are always welcome.

Then we found our way to the Jesuits' Church, where there was uncovered a silver statue of Loyola, of priceless value for the gems set in it, and the masses of lapis lazuli.

Afterwards, we sat on the Pincian till the rain came, and it has poured down ever since, making our journey to this place a more weary one than usual. Everything is shrouded in mist, mildewed and funereal, except the young waterfalls, which leap like lions' whelps from Bashan, and laugh, and fling themselves about in their glee.

๛๛๛๛

Genoa.—We left Florence on Friday, and the day was fine, so that we greatly enjoyed the journey over the mountains to Bologna. Then it is a dull road to Alessandria, which we reached about six o'clock. Thence to Genoa should take two hours and a-half; but, in ascending the Maritime Alps, there was snow, and the engine crawled along, and at last stopped altogether. Think of it,—going uphill, and stopping!

The steam was put on, and the wheels revolved, sending out a shower of sparks, but the train did not stir. Then came men with spades to clear away some snow, and after a while the carriages moved, we gained the top of the hill, and ran down all right, getting into Genoa about 10 p.m.

A long, tiresome day.

Here, where we were so comfortable last year, we were marched up four sets of stairs, and then shown into rooms which had a most offensive smell. The house was full, the waiter said, and they could give us no other rooms. We replied, 'Very well, then, we will go somewhere else;' and when we had carried all our luggage to the door, apartments were found for us on the first floor!

A view of Genoa, from the travel book *Italie*, by Artaud (1835).

This morning, expecting to leave for Mentone at twelve o'clock, we hear that the line is broken in four places, and no train goes except at eight a.m., so we are here till Monday. It rains, and has rained all night in torrents.

We must wait, and then go on in great uncertainty and sure discomfort. Never mind! it will serve me for illustration, no doubt. Dr. Jobson, a Wesleyan minister, has had an hour's happy chat with me, and very much interested me. He is a holy, liberal-hearted soul, and we enjoy a conversation together, so it is not all dulness.

It is beginning to clear up while I am writing, so perhaps we may get a walk.

I have had restful nights this week, and am still really much better, but the damp and cold try me a good deal.

❧❦❧❦

Sabbath.—This day, which we have been forced to spend here, has not been an unhappy one, but a sweet day, most calm and bright. The rain cleared off yesterday about four o'clock, enabling us to wander through the narrow streets of Genoa la Superba, and to enter several of the churches. My indignation was stirred beyond measure when, upon looking into the confessional boxes, I read the directions to the priest as to the questions he should ask the penitents. These were printed in Latin, and referred to those unmentionable crimes which brought fire upon Sodom, and are the curse of heathendom.

To see young maidens kneel down to be asked such questions as these …

Since I came away, my more sober reflections fully endorse my indignant wrath. How can the Lord endure all this? Truly, His patience is great.

ৡৢৢৢ

To-day we had our breaking of bread, and Dr. Jobson and his wife joined us.

The good old man spoke most sweetly, and prayed for you with great pathos, and much faith that the Lord would yet heal you. He shamed me by his faith, and I blessed him for his tender affection. The Lord was with us, and the season will be memorable to us all.

Then I revised a sermon, which is not quite finished yet; but the table d'hote bell is ringing, so I must needs pause a while, and allow the body to feed in its turn.

To-day is fine and bright, and has been warm in the sun. We have large leads to walk on, and I have had a little turn there while the others have gone up on the heights for a walk.

To-morrow, I hope, will be equally clear, and then we shall not mind the getting out and in where the railway is broken.

ৡৢৢৢ

Table d'hote is now over, and I have had the old Doctor in for a talk, though I wanted to be alone, and go on with my sermon and letters. However, the good soul is gone now, and I can get to my dear work of communing with my darling by the pen.

Every memory of you is full of joy, except your illness; and that makes me love you all the more, by adding sympathy. I am afraid I am still a rough, forgetful being, so apt to get absorbed in my work, and to think too little of you; but this is not in my heart, but is in my nature; and I suppose, if it were not there, I could not do my work so successfully.

You know and love me too well to judge as others would. We have to be off early in the morning, so I must close this note.

৯৵৵৵৵

Mentone.—We came here yesterday from Genoa, and a very interesting journey it was. We left Genoa at eight o'clock, and went on all right till ten, when we all had to get out, for the road was destroyed. We walked down a lane, then over a bridge, then down on the other side, and up the embankment, and got into another train. In this case, the bridge of the railway was broken by a torrent, and a break indeed it was. In due time, we went on; but, in an hour or so, came to a dead halt, and had to get out again.

This time the walk was long, and the way went through a vineyard, and up a steep bank. Crowds of men and boys clamoured for our luggage, and followed us all the half-mile we had to trudge. We had to wait forty minutes till another train came; and then, when we scrambled in, they quietly shoved us out of the way, and made us sit still for forty minutes more. We went on a little, only to stop again; and, at last, at Porto Maurizio, we had the carriages pushed by men over a dangerous place, and then hooked on to another train.

However, we reached Ventimiglia safely at about seven o'clock, and then had an hour to wait to have dinner. We left there at 8 p.m., and arrived here at 7:20 p.m., this last being the greatest feat I ever performed! To travel for twenty minutes, and then to find the clock forty minutes behind the time at which you started, is a gain not to be despised;—the explanation is that Roman time is used at Ventimiglia, and Paris time at Mentone.

Mentone seen from Dr Bennet's garden, and as published in the *Authobiobraphy (*1899).

The day was fine, and though the way was long, the adventures made the hours pass away merrily, and our Mark Tapley friend was quite in his element. We are at a most comfortable hotel, and everyone tries to please us. The landlord knew me at once, and shook hands heartily, saying, 'How do you do, reverend? I am very glad to see you!'

৯৶৶৶

To-day, while I was lying on the beach, and Mark Tapley was slyly filling our pockets with stones, and rolling Mr. Passmore over, who should walk up but Mr. McLaren, of Manchester, with whom I had a long and pleasant chat.

We are to go to Monaco to-morrow together. He has three months' holiday.

I am glad I have not; but I should wish I had, if I had my dear wife with me to enjoy it. Poor little soul! she must suffer while I ramble.

Two clergymen have had a long talk with me this evening. It began by one saying aloud to the other, 'I hear Mr. Spurgeon has been here.' This caused a titter round the table, for I was sitting opposite to him. Mentone is charming, but not very warm.

It is as I like it, and is calculated to make a sick man leap with health.

How I wish you could be here!

৯৶৶৶

We have had another day here of the sweetest rest. We drove to Monaco and back, and saw to perfection the little rocky Principality. Its lovely gardens and promenades are kept up by the profits of the gaming-tables, which are in a far more sumptuous palace than those at Baden-Baden, which we saw together years ago.

We had Mr. McLaren with us, and went in and watched the players. One gentleman monopolized our attention; he was a fine-looking Englishman, like an officer. He lost a pile of money, and went out apparently most wretched and excited.

Soon, he came in again, and changed bills for 3,000 francs, and began playing heavily, he won, and got back his bills; and when we left, we saw him come out; I could only hope that God had delivered him, and that he would be wise, and never go to the table again. It is a vortex which sucks in a vast number of victims day by day.

What moths men are if the candle be but bright enough!

ॐॐॐ

The two parsons here are High Church and Low Church, and I have had a talk with both. Just before dinner, who should go by but the Earl of Shaftesbury, with whom I had half-an-hour's converse. He was very low in spirit, and talked as if all things in the world were going wrong; but I reminded him that our God was yet alive, and that dark days were only the signs of better times coming. He is a real nobleman, and man of God.

Everybody in the hotel is courteous and kind, and I have quite a circle of acquaintances already. I have enjoyed the rest very much; but young married couples remind me of our early days, and the cloud which covers us now.

Still, He who sent both sun and shade is our ever-tender Father, and knows best; and if it be good for us, He can restore all that He has withdrawn, and more; and if not, He designs our yet greater good. There is nothing more to write, except the ever true and never tiresome message,—my perfect love be with thee, and the Lord's love be over thee for ever!

In a few more days I shall see thee, and it will be a fairer sight than any my eyes have rested on during my absence.

Yesterday, Mr. and Mrs. Müller went with me to Dr. Bennet's garden, and I had a most profitable conversation with him, one to be remembered for many a day with delight. Dr. Bennet came up, and I was amused to hear Müller teaching him the power of prayer, and recommending him to pray about one of the terraces which he wants to buy, but the owner asks a hundred times its value.

George Müller, as shown in W.H. Harding's biography (1914).

Dr. B. thought it too trifling a matter to take to the Lord; he said that Mr. Müller might very properly pray about the Orphanage, but as to this terrace, to complete his garden,—he thought he could not make out a good case about it. Mr. M. said it encouraged people in sin if we yielded to covetous demands, so he thought the Dr. might pray that the owners should be kept from exorbitant claims ...

The spirit of both was good; but, of course, the simple, child-like holy trust of Müller was overpowering. He is not a sanctimonious person; but full of real joy, and sweet peace, and innocent pleasure.

Nice.—In this place we have been put up four flights of stairs, and, alas! into very cold rooms. I woke in the night, and felt as if I were freezing in a vault, and my ankles were in great pain. I was much cast down; and, on getting out of bed, found the carpet and floor both very damp. I had a very bad night, and am now in much pain in the left foot.

Yet I believe I shall get over it soon, and I mean to have no more of these climbings up stairs, and sleeping in horrid cells.

Nice is a very grand place, and I am sorry we left Mentone to come to it.

But I must not write in a grumbling vein. Here have I had nearly five weeks of good health, and have grown stronger every day; why should I care for one little relapse? We will be off to Cannes and Hyeres, and see what God has in store for us. He will deal graciously with me as He has ever done.

❧☙☙❧

Cannes.—I was too ill yesterday to write. After the deadly chill of Thursday night at Nice, I felt the gout coming on, but resolved to escape from that inhospitable hotel.

An hour brought us here, but it rained mercilessly, and all around was damp and chill. I got upstairs into beautiful rooms, but had to go to bed, which I have only left for a moment or two since, while it was being arranged. My left foot is badly swollen, and the knee-joint is following suit. I have had very little sleep, and am very low; but, oh, the kindness of these friends! They sit up with me all night by turns, and cheer me with promises.

I hope I shall get home in time for Sunday, but have some fears of it. Do not fret about me, I may be well before this reaches you; and if I am, I will telegraph and say so.

I have every comfort here but home, and my dear wifey's sweet words. I am sad that my journey should end so, but the Lord's will be done!

❧☙☙❧

Two days later.—I have had a heavy time of pain, my dearest, but am now better. God has changed the weather;—yesterday was warm, to-day is hot, so we think it best to hurry on, and, if possible, have a *coupé-lit* right through to Paris.

I feel well in myself, but the knee will not bear me, though I think I should be as strong as a horse after a day or two of this weather. How much I have to thank the Lord for! Such kind friends! They have proved their love

131

beyond all praise. I was never alone. Even the femme de chambre pitied 'pauvre monsieur,' and did her best for me.

I hope now to get home in time for Sunday. My soul loves you, and longs to see you.

> Bless the Lord, O my soul; and may He bless thee, too, my dear heart of love … I am indeed grateful to God for His goodness; still, 'there's no place like home.' This brings great loads of love all flaming. God bless thee ever!

Susannah Spurgeon in early married life, from the *Autobiography*, vol. 2 (1898).

✥ APPENDIX 1 ✥
'Lessons from Nature,' selected lines
from Spurgeon's sermon of 12th August, 1871

'Where the birds make their nests: as for the stork, the fir trees are her house. The high hills are a refuge for the wild goats, and the rooks for the conies.'
—Psalm 104:17-18

EDITOR'S NOTE: This sermon relates in many ways to the themes and reflections Spurgeon touched on in letters to his wife Susannah during his holiday in England, 1873.

Rest, recreation, and time amid places of God's creation—all are blessings. Indeed, there are telling lessons in the book of nature God has written.

And this sermon may be seen as a Spurgeon 'letter' of another kind—save that it was 'written,' or rather given, to a congregation instead of a letter home to family.

Seen in this light, it is a true companion piece to the letters Susannah Spurgeon included from her husband in the pages of his Autobiography. Here, Spurgeon begins—

This Psalm [the 104th,] is all through a song of nature, the adoration of God in the great outward temple of the universe.

Some in these modern times have thought it to be a mark of high spirituality never to observe nature; and I remember sorrowfully reading the expressions of a godly person, who, in sailing down one of the most famous rivers in the world, closed his eyes, lest the picturesque beauties of the scene should divert his mind from scriptural topics.

This may be regarded by some as profound spirituality; to me it seems to savour of absurdity. There may be persons who think they have grown in grace when they have attained to this; it seems to me that they are growing out of their senses. To despise the creating work of God, what is it but, in a measure, to despise God himself?

❧❧❧❧

… to think little of God under the aspect of the Creator is a crime. We should none of us think it a great honour to ourselves if our friends considered our productions to be unworthy of admiration, and rather injurious to their minds than improving.

If, when they passed our workmanship, they turned their eyes away, lest they should suffer injury by looking at it, we should not regard them as very respectful to ourselves; surely the despising of that which is made, is somewhat akin to the despising of the Maker himself.

David tells us that 'The Lord shall rejoice in His works.' If He rejoices in what He has made, shall not those who have communion with Him rejoice in His works also?

৩৽৶৶৶

… this prejudice against the beauties of the material universe reminds me of [that] which acted like a spell upon Peter of old. When the sheet knit at the four corners descended before him, and the voice said, 'Rise, Peter; kill, and eat,' he replied that he had not eaten anything that was common or unclean. He needed that the voice should speak to him from heaven again and again before he would fully learn the lesson,

'What God hath cleansed … call not … [unclean].'

৩৽৶৶৶

… certain Christians appear to regard nature as unclean.

The birds of the air, and the fish of the sea, the glorious sunrise and sunset, the snow-clad Alps, the ancient forests, the mysterious glaciers, the boundless ocean, God hath cleansed them: call them not common …

৩৽৶৶৶

Rest assured brethren, that He who wrote the Bible, the second and clearest revelation of His divine mind, wrote also the first book, the book of nature; and who are we that we should derogate from the worth of the first, because we esteem the second.

Milton's Paradise Regained is certainly inferior to his Paradise Lost, but the Eternal God has no inferior productions, all His works are master-pieces.

There is no quarrel between nature and revelation, fools only think so: to wise men the one illustrates and establishes the other. Walking in the fields at eventide, as Isaac did, I see in the ripening harvest the same God, of whom I read in the Word, that He covenanted that seed-time and harvest should not cease. Surveying the midnight skies, I remember Him who, while He calls the stars by their names, also bindeth up the broken in heart.

[Some] may neglect the volume of creation, or the volume of revelation:

I shall delight in them both as long as I live.

Let us, then, follow David this morning, for when he wrote our text, he evidently travelled amongst the works of God, admiring and adoring.

Let us go with him, and see if there be not something to be learned among the birds and storks, the wild goats and the conies.

᪇᪇᪇᪇

Almost every part of God's world was meant to be the abode of some creature or another. On earth, a countless company wait upon the Lord for meat; and as for the sea, it contains 'creeping things innumerable, both small and great beasts.'

Among the trees which shade the brooks, the birds are singing; in the tall sombre pine, the silent storks are building their nests; on the lofty crags, virgin as yet to human foot, the chamois leaps from ledge to ledge; and away, where human voice was never heard, the marmot, the mouse, and the rabbit ...find their dwelling-place among the rocks ...

ঙ৹৵৵৹

Birds with their nests for the cedars of Lebanon, storks for the fir trees, wild goats for the high hills, and conies for the rocks. Each of these creatures looks most beautiful at home.

Go into the Zoological Gardens, and see the poor animals there under artificial conditions, and you can little guess what they are at home.

A lion in a cage is a very different creature from a lion in the wilderness. The stork looks wretched in his wire pen, and you would hardly know him as the same creature if you saw him on the housetops or on the fir trees. Each creature looks best in its own place.

Take that truth now, and use it for yourself. Each man has by God a providential position appointed to him, and the position ordained for each Christian is that in which he looks best; it is the best for him, and he is the best for that; and if you could change his position, and shift him to another, he would not be half as happy, nor half as useful, nor half so much himself.

ঙ৹৵৵৹

Now, briefly, a third point ...

Birds fly to the trees, and the stork to the fir, the wild goat to the high hills, and the coney to the rocks. There is a shelter for every one of these creatures, great and small. Think a moment, then, if God has made each creature happy, and given a place of refuge to each creature, then, depend upon it, He has not left man's soul without a shelter.

ৡৢৡৢৡ

And now ... the fourth observation, that for each creature the shelter is appropriate.

The tree for the bird; the fir tree, a particular and special tree, for the stork; a high hill for the steinbock or ibex, and the rocks for the hyrax or rabbit. Whatever creature it may be, each shall have his own suitable shelter.

But, you will reply to me, is there a shelter then, for each individual man? Did you not say that there was only one shelter for manhood?

If I did not say it, I certainly will say it now.

There is only one shelter under heaven or in heaven for any man of woman born, but yet there is a shelter suitable for each. Christ Jesus suits all sorts of sinners, all sorts of sufferers. He is a Saviour as suitable for me as if He came to save me and no one else; but He is a Redeemer as remarkably suitable to every other of His redeemed ones.

Note, then, that there is a refuge in Christ Jesus for those simple trustful natures that take the gospel at once and believe it. These are like the little birds that fly to the trees and build their nests and begin to sing. These are the commonest sort of Christians, but in some respects they are the best. They hear the gospel, believe it to be God's word, accept it, and begin to sing. Jesus Christ exactly suits them, He is a shelter for those chosen birds of the air, whom your heavenly Father daily feeds.

But there are others of larger intellect, who require unusual support ere they can build their nest and be at ease.

These, like the stork, need a special support, and they find it in the gospel. Since they are more weighty with doubt and perplexity, they need substantial verities to rest on; these find great fir-tree doctrines, and cedar-like principles in the Bible, and they rest in them.

Many of us this day are resting on the immutable things wherein it is impossible for God to lie. We rest upon the substitution of Christ, and repose in the completeness of the atonement. Some get hold of one great principle and some another in connection with the grace of God; and God has been pleased to reveal strong, immovable, eternal, immutable principles in His Word, which are suitable for thoughtful and troubled minds to rest on.

Moreover, we have in the church of God persons of great reasoning powers: these love the craggy paths of thought, but when they come to Christ and trust in Him, though they are like the wild goat and love the high places, they find in the Scriptures good ground for them ...

෴෴෴

Now we must close ... with this observation, that each creature uses its shelter, for the storks have made their nests in the fir trees, and the wild goats climb the high hills, and the conies hide among the rocks. I never heard of one of these creatures that neglected its shelter— they love their natural abodes; but I have heard of men who have neglected their God, I know women who have forgotten Christ. We say, 'silly sheep.'

Ah, if the sheep knew all about us, they would wonder we should call them silly.

The coney in danger which does not seek its rock is foolish; but the soul in danger which does not seek its Saviour is insane—insane, nay, if there can be a madness which is as much beyond madness, as madness is beyond sanity, then such is the raving lunacy of a man who neglects the Saviour.

I have never heard of any of these creatures that they despise the shelter provided. The birds are satisfied with the trees, and the stork with the firs, and even the coney with its rock-hole; but, alas! there are men who despise Christ.

God himself becomes the shelter of sinners, and yet sinners despise their God.

The Son of God opens His side, and lays bare His heart, that a soul may come and shelter there in the crimson cleft, and yet that soul for many a day refuses to accept the shelter. Oh, where are tears? Who shall give us fit expressions for our sorrow that men should be such monsters to themselves, and to their God?

The ox knoweth its owner, and the ass its master's crib; but men know not God. The stork knows its fir tree, the wild goat its crag, and the coney knows its cleft, but the sinner knows not his Christ. Ah, manhood, what has befallen thee?

What strange wine of Gomorrah ... has thus intoxicated thee!

One other thing, I never heard of a stork that when it met with a fir tree demurred as to its right to build its nest there, and I never heard of a coney yet that questioned whether it had a permit to run into the rock. Why these creatures would soon perish if they were always doubting and fearing as to whether they had a right to use providential provisions.

The stork says to himself, 'Ah, here is a fir tree;' he consults with his mate—'Will this do for the nest in which we may rear our young?'

'Ay' says she, and they gather the materials, and arrange them. There is never any deliberation, 'May we build here?' but they bring their sticks and make their nest.

So the wild goat on the crag does not say, 'Have I a right to be here?' No, he must be somewhere, and there is a crag which exactly suits him; and he springs upon it. Yet though these dumb creatures know the provision of their God, the sinner does not recognize the provisions of his Saviour. He quibbles and questions, 'May I?' and 'I am afraid it is not for me,' and 'I think it cannot be meant for me; and I am afraid it is too good to be true.'

And yet nobody ever said to the stork, 'Whosoever buildeth on this fir tree shall never have his nest pulled down.' No inspired word has ever said to the coney, 'Whosoever runs into this rock-cleft shall never be driven out of it;' if it had been so, it would make assurance doubly sure. And yet here is Christ provided for sinners, just the sort of a Saviour sinners need, and the encouragement is added, 'Him that cometh unto me I will in no wise cast out;' 'Whosoever will, let him come, and take the water of life freely.'

O dear brothers and sisters, do not be standing out against the generosity of a sin-pardoning God, who bids the sinner come and welcome. Come, believe in Jesus, and find salvation now. O that you would come, it is what God has provided for your wants.

Come, take it, for He bids you come. 'The Spirit and the bride say come, and whosoever will, let him come and take the water of life freely.'

To believe is to trust Jesus, to trust His suffering, to trust His atonement, and rely upon Him alone for salvation. May God enable you to do it for Christ's sake. Amen.

❧ APPENDIX 2 ❧
Lines from the article,
'From England to Italy: A Chapter from the Book of Nature',
by C.H. Spurgeon: from the June 1865 issue of *The Sword and the Trowel* magazine.

EDITOR'S NOTE: Spurgeon's common practise as a magazine editor was to write with the authorial 'we,' that is to say, in the second person voice.

So, in the article lines that follow, Spurgeon is talking about himself, and his own experiences. Time in Europe stirred his thoughts about gifts God gave in Creation. In his travels, he saw all these 'wonders in nature,' as he called them, with deep gratitude.

And now, to his reflections …

In a few days we have left our white-cliffed island, crossed the Channel, traversed France, penetrated the heart of Switzerland, passed the Alps, and entered sunny Italy.

We have seen a thousand things, and mused upon ten thousand more; and our thoughts, like the fishes in the blue lake which sparkles at our feet, are very many …

The Great Master Author has sent forth several volumes; among the rest is one called the 'Book of Revelation,' and another styled the 'Volume of Creation.'

We have been reading the Word-volume, and expounding it for years, we are now perusing the Work-volume, and are engrossed in some of its most glowing pages.

Our love for the sacred book of letters and words has not diminished but increased our admiration for the hieroglyphics of the flood and field. That man perversely mistakes folly for wisdom who persists in undervaluing one glorious poem, by a famous author, in order to show his zeal for a second epic from the same fertile pen. [So I say:]

> It is the mark of a feeble mind to despise the wonders of nature, because we prize the treasures of salvation.

He who built the lofty skies is as much our Father as He who hath spoken to us by his own Son, and we should reverently adore HIM who in creation decketh himself with majesty and excellency, even as in revelation HE arrayeth himself in glory and beauty.

৽৵৵৽

Modern fanatics, who profess to be so absorbed in heavenly things that they are blind to the most marvellous of Jehovah's handiwork, should go to school—with David as the schoolmaster, and learn to 'consider the heavens,' and should sit with Job upon the dunghill of their pride, while the Lord rehearses the thundering stanzas of creation's greatness, until they cry with the patriarch, 'I have heard of Thee by the hearing of the ear, but now mine eye seeth Thee; wherefore I abhor myself, and repent in dust and ashes.'

ক্ষ্মেক্ষ্

For our part, we feel that what was worth the Lord's making richly deserves the attention of the most cultivated and purified intellect; and we think it blasphemy against God Himself to speak slightingly of His universe—as if, forsooth—we poor puny mortals were too spiritual to be interested in that matchless architecture which made the morning stars sing together, and caused the sons of God to shout for joy.

ক্ষ্মেক্ষ্

Our hasty perusal of one short chapter of the book of nature has sufficed to assure us that its author most certainly wrote the Holy Scriptures.

Writers have their own idiomatic expressions and modes of thought; kings of literature set their image and superscription upon the coinage of their minds; and therefore you can detect a literary forgery as readily as a counterfeit bank note.

The paintings of the old masters may be cleverly copied, but the man of taste would soon discover the imposture, if a mere copy were palmed upon him as the original; a certain indescribable something would be wanting, and there would be present a tint, a manner, or an expression quite unknown to the master's purer style.

In the productions of 'the Great Artist,' the rule holds good.

Deity has a peculiar manner which it is quite impossible to imitate with success ...

ശ്ശഗ

We observe this same quality in nature.

How great the difference between yonder granite mountain and the cloud which caps it; the raging wind, and the bright star which smiles serenely amid the storm; the cataract which leaps from rock to rock, and the solitude through which it roars; the boundless ocean, and the grain of sand which lies on its shore!

In a few hours [of travel,] we climbed from fields of corn to slopes of snow, through which our road was cut at a depth of ten or twenty feet; and before the sun had set, we were in sultry plains, where figs and grapes grow in rich profusion ...

Variety was there indeed, for no two scenes were the same, yet the unity was equally conspicuous, for who could fail to see that the floating cloud feeds the foaming cataract with its descending deluge, that the rivers bind the mountains to the ocean by silver cords, and that winds, and waves, and mists, and stars, and Alps, are all wheels of the same great machinery. From the garden of figs, up through the chestnut grove, to the pine forest, and yet higher to the fair blue gentian, the modest moss, and the blackened lichen, and highest of all to the eternal snow, seems a long ascent of infinite variety; but, as the stones of a geometrical staircase all rest on one another, so do all the ranks of vegetable life, so that the blue-bells and red rhododendrons, which blush unseen far up in some sunny crevice, are as necessary parts of the whole fabric as the golden wheat-sheaf, and the luxuriant vine.

৯৵৵৹

The departments of animate and inanimate nature are but the various books of the great Bible of Creation, and their teaching is one and harmonious ...

Such strange blendings of grandeur and gentleness we have seen all this week. Amidst a thick fog in crossing the Channel, which clothed everything in mystery, and made us grope our way with anxious tardiness, we heard the cries of sea-birds; they at least had not lost their way; come mist or rain, the God of the floods had numbered every one of their feathers, and given them joys far out on the deep of which the prophet says, 'There is sorrow on the sea.'

৯৵৵৹

Seeing the jonquil, the hyacinth, the anemone, and many others of our garden flowers growing wild in the valleys on the Italian side of the Alps, and hearing the ceaseless chirping of the innumerable insects which fill the air with their song, and looking up to the snowy peaks piercing the clouds, one could not help comparing the beauty and perfectness of the little, with the overwhelming awe and sublimity of the great.

He who launches the thunderbolt guides the fire-fly; He who hurls the falling mass from the shivering alpine summit controls the descent of the dew-drop; and He, who covereth heaven and earth with the black wings of tempest, stoops down to cherish the violet blooming amid the velvet turf ...

৯০৵৵৵

As we were sitting by the Lake of Lucerne, the rugged old Pilatus was suddenly covered with blackness, forth flashed the forked lightning, followed by sharp cracks of thunder, reverberated in long peals—enough to let us know that the artillery of heaven had not spent its might, and that the arsenals of the storm were as fully stored as ever ...

Yet as we looked around and saw the sun smiling forth again over the glorious hills, his beams flashing brightly upon the countless wavelets of the lake, vegetation freshened by the newly fallen shower, glistening with rain drops as with sparkling diamonds, and man and beast rejoicing in the clear shining and the cool air, we could not but feel that the stern Lord of Tempests was infinitely kind ... Our week's wanderings have taught us ...

ৡৡৡৡ

Sing the verses of some fine old psalm in a pine forest, in a boat on the blue waves, on the summit of an Alp, in a dark defile, or in the hollow of a great rock, and see if they do not give a tongue to all around, and prove man to be the soul of all things ...

Forgive me, dear readers, if, as a man seeking rest, I drop the pen, and go forth from my chamber to gaze, and gaze again, on loveliness. Would you know what I have gazed upon to-day and yesterday, these lines which I find in Murray's Handbook ... will possibly suggest more than I can write of Italian hills and scenery—

> Sublime, but neither bleak nor bare,
> Nor misty, are the mountains there,—
> Softly sublime, profusely fair!
>
> Up to their summits clothed in green,
> And fruitful as the vales between,
> They lightly rise
> And scale the skies,
> And groves and gardens still abound,
> For where no shoot
> could else take root,
> The peaks are shelved, and terraced round;
> Earthward appear in mingled growth
> The mulberry and maize,—above,
> the trellised vine extends to both
> The leafy shade they love.

Looks out the white-wall'd cottage here;
The lowly chapel rises near;
Far down the foot must roam to reach
The lovely lake and bending beach;
While chestnut green and olive gray,
Chequer the steep and winding way.[1]
[— Henry Taylor]

1. See *A Handbook for Travellers in Switzerland, and the Alps of Savoy and Piedmont* (London: John Murray, 1865), 319. Most often, this book was called simply by its nickname, 'Murray's Handbook,' which appears on the cover of this red-book edition. It was a standard text, hence Spurgeon's use and referral to it.